S0-ADQ-533

The Cross Is Still Mightier Than the Switchblade

The Cross Is Still Mightier Than the Switchblade

Don Wilkerson

© Copyright 1996 — Don Wilkerson

All rights reserved. This book is protected under the copyright laws of the United States of America. This book may not be copied or reprinted for commercial gain or profit. The use of short quotations or occasional page copying for personal or group study is permitted and encouraged. Permission will be granted upon request. Unless otherwise identified, Scripture quotations are from the King James Version of the Bible. Scripture quotations marked (NIV) and (NAS) are taken from the New International Version and the New American Standard, respectively. Emphasis within Scripture is the author's own.

Take note that the name satan and related names are not capitalized. We choose not to acknowledge him, even to the point of violating grammatical rules.

Treasure House

An Imprint of
Destiny Image® Publishers, Inc.
P.O. Box 310
Shippensburg, PA 17257-0310

"For where your treasure is,
there will your heart be also." Matthew 6:21

ISBN 1-56043-264-0

Fourth Printing: 1998   Fifth Printing: 2000

For Worldwide Distribution
Printed in the U.S.A.

This book and all other Destiny Image,
Revival Press, Mercy Place, Fresh Bread,
and Treasure House books are available at
Christian bookstores and distributors worldwide.

For a U.S. bookstore nearest you, call **1-800-722-6774**.
For more information on foreign distributors,
call **1-717-532-3040**.
Or reach us on the Internet: **http://www.reapernet.com**

Endorsements

"I sincerely appreciate your efforts to reach and rehabilitate the many young people who, in the present, have no hope in life. The work and dedication of the staff of Teen Challenge deserve the commendation of every citizen."

Ronald Reagan

"...of all the programs reported to the commission, the most successful is the religiously based program conducted by Teen Challenge."

Dr. John A. Howard
National Commission on Marijuana
and Drug Abuse

"In my opinion, Teen Challenge is doing the best all-around job of providing kids with something meaningful in their lives. And that's what they need."

Art Linkletter

"I believe in the work of this great organization. A government-funded research project concluded that Teen Challenge has the highest success rate in helping people move from substance abuse, off substance abuse."

John Ashcroft
U.S. Senator

Contents

Foreword

I had no idea, when I picked up that paperback with the intriguing title *The Cross and the Switchblade* from the airport newsstand in 1969, that my life would never be the same after I read it.

After I put the finished book down, wiped away my tears, and allowed the supernatural goose bumps all over my body to subside, I vowed to reach Dave Wilkerson, through whatever means necessary. I wanted to find out two things: (a) were all these things true as he described them, and (b) might we discuss making a movie of this incredible story?

When I got back to Los Angeles, I obtained a number in New York for David Wilkerson and got him on the phone. He was crisp and direct, perhaps even a little wary (he didn't have much regard for people in show business, and still doesn't). To my first question he answered, with just a little apparent irritation, "Do you think I'd lie about these things? If God hadn't miraculously protected and led me, I'd have been dead a long time ago."

He seemed no more responsive to my idea about making a movie. Little did I know that in *his* church background, even *going* to movies was frowned on! Still, we met in New York eventually, with his board of advisors, and agreed to commit the concept to the Lord.

Well, many miracles later, the movie was filmed in the very streets of Harlem, Fort Green, and Little Puerto Rico where David actually lived the story and confronted the street gangs, and where Teen Challenge was founded. I had the frightening privilege of playing Dave Wilkerson, and I and the whole movie company were totally dependent on God's protection as we *filmed*, just as David and his few friends were when he *lived* it the first time! The police begged us not to go into those streets, and assured us they could not protect us from the same gangs and violence that had confronted Dave in the beginning.

Through that whole spine-tingling experience, my life was changed. When your life is literally at risk, day after day, when you're involved in a task that is humanly impossible, when the forces of hell are arrayed against you in many insidious forms—and when even the police desert you—you learn about the immediacy and power of prayer, and how real God is.

That's the story of Teen Challenge from day one.

The title isn't just a cute gimmick, an effort to sell a book. The cross and the switchblade meet daily in the inner cities of our country, and in a huge majority of cases, the cross still wins!

All that happens in Teen Challenge without any government subsidy, and in a constant struggle for just the minimum dollars required to keep facilities open and a skeleton staff in food and lodging. As you'll read in the following pages, though responsible people in the government *know this is the only program that works, at an over 70 percent cure rate,* they feel that our courts and tragic misinterpretations of the Constitution regarding "separation of Church and State" prohibit any government funding for the one proven answer to America's giant drug and crime problem.

And so the story continues. I'm very grateful to Don Wilkerson, the author, for documenting the next two decades of the Teen Challenge living drama. Again, it reads like additional chapters in the Book of Acts! Over the many years since I played Dave Wilkerson in the alleys and gang rooms of upper New York City, I've had many occasions to visit the Teen Challenge Centers across the country and to participate in a number of fund-raising activities. It seems so wrong to me that these good people, who are out on the very front lines fighting drugs, crime, and violence so successfully, have to operate almost continually on practically no budget. We, Christians and non-Christians alike, as grateful American citizens, need to lavishly support this wonderfully effective program.

As you read this gripping tale, you'll be caught up in the same tears and goose bumps that afflicted me originally, and I hope you'll make the same commitment to supporting Teen Challenge that I have.

Pat Boone

Chapter 1

The Cross Is Still Mightier Than the Switchblade

The sign outside the entrance of the inner-city Los Angeles courtyard read:

BE IT KNOWN: These are NEUTRAL GROUNDS Guarded by Angels through the Power of the Holy Spirit by Direct Order of Jesus of Nazareth; therefore: NO WEAPONS, DRUGS, TOBACCO, PROFANITY, GAMBLING, OR FIGHTING ALLOWED.

This "neutral ground" is the Los Angeles County Teen Challenge Center in the heart of L.A. Two important things happen at that center. The first is the center's weekly ministry to local Latino gangs like the "Oak Street Chips," the "Lynwood Mob," the "Banning Street Gang," and "El Segundo," among many others.

Each week hundreds of local toughs pass by that sign for those meetings. The regulars all know they are entering "God's turf," so they hide their weapons elsewhere. Since newcomers come every week, who don't know the ropes yet, everyone is "patted down" for weapons before entering the premises—just to be safe.

The "homies" who pass by the sign onto the "neutral turf" each week find a large full-sized basketball court, a handball court, weight training gear, and other recreational equipment waiting for them. After a few hours of sports activities, the regulars know things are about to get serious—real serious. They know they will face the challenge of their lives in the simple service that follows, because they will all be confronted with the gospel. Even the newcomers know it's time to shut out the gang world outside and *listen*.

Oddly enough, these tough young gang members *do* listen! This remarkable event is a welcome contrast to the violence, fighting, and killing that goes on beyond the safety of the Teen Challenge Center's "neutral ground." They gladly listen to the testimonies of former gang members and drug addicts, and the short salvation message that always follows. On "God's turf," the issue is life and death of another kind—will they choose eternal life or eternal death?

Perhaps for the first time in their lives, these gang members hear about a Power that is greater than any gang, drug, chemical rush, sexual experience, or gang brotherhood. As one speaker at the center said, "There has already been enough blood shed around here, but it is because of the shed blood of Jesus that lives will be changed in this place!"

The second event takes place at a Teen Challenge house where gang members, drug addicts, alcoholics, and convicted criminals enter a resident discipling program to discover a new way of life through the message of the Bible and the person of Jesus Christ. The converts who come to Christ at the center become living examples to those still in the gangs, demonstrating before their eyes that they too can be saved from their living hell and receive a new and exciting life. These changed lives are a sobering reality that is hard to deny.

Gang members reached through the weekly meetings in Los Angeles County (where there are 90,000 members in some 900 organized gangs), and in Orange County (which is nearly as bad), are offered the chance to go on summer camp retreats conducted by Teen Challenge in the San Bernardino Mountains. These summer camps provide even more serious life-changing ministry to nearly 100 gang members each camp session. Just the fact that so many gang members from different gangs can come together without bloodshed is a miracle—especially since many of them belong to rival gangs trapped in a vicious cycle of inter-gang hatred and violence!

Once when a Teen Challenge worker drove up to a gang member's house expecting to take him to summer camp, he realized the boy was being arrested! After the worker told the arresting officer about the Christian camp, the policeman looked at the gang member and said, "You need to go to this camp more than you need to go to jail." Then he removed the handcuffs and released the teen to the Teen Challenge worker!

The Teen Challenge camp is different from the summer camps many of us remember from our childhood. During the first few days of the camp, these unusual "campers" continue to act out their tough roles because both male and female gang members feel they need to maintain the "gang" image they work so hard to maintain on the streets. None of them can envision what will happen in the days to follow as the Spirit of God begins to break down the walls of hate and despair that imprison these young people.

Everyone attends chapel for an hour-and-a-half twice a day throughout the weeklong retreat. As the Holy Spirit begins His work, the young people will actually learn to pray and worship God. By mid-week, most of the gang members are starting to remain seated in the chapel long after the meeting has ended—there is something or Someone who makes them want to linger there. Then the services begin to last four or five hours as more and more gang members are reborn as disciples of Jesus Christ.

"I never saw so many tears in my life," said Robert Calderon, one of the leaders who described a recent meeting to me. "It seems like all the hardness melts away as they pray on their knees in the chapel. They cry and cry for hours!" Calderon said. "Once they realize that God is real and that He loves them, they respond and get their hearts right with Him. Then, it seems like they are immediately burdened for all their fellow gang members back home who still don't know about God's great love."

In most instances, more than half of the gang members who attend the camp accept Christ. Jesse was a 13-year-old gang member (13 is no longer considered "young" in today's gang culture) who accepted Jesus at a Teen Challenge camp. He wrote our staff a letter when he got back home to share his testimony (reproduced here complete with Jesse's original spelling):

"I liked the servises alot. I tried not to cry but I coudn'ent stop crying. I could fill Jesus love in the room. I just rote this to tell you guys Thanks."

Jesse's conversion is extraordinary because he, and every other gang member who comes to Jesus, knows what that commitment will mean to them personally. They know their decision could cost them dearly once they reenter their daily environment of war zone shootings, gang murder, drugs, and all the other hellish circumstances of inner-city gang life.

When the camping retreat ends, new converts can join a new gang called "God's Gang," consisting of converted gang members and drug addicts who want to join the Teen Challenge Club. This club was set up for those willing to be true disciples of Christ, and it provides them with other organized recreational and spiritual ministry opportunities on weekends in addition to the weekly meetings at the center. More than 400 teens belonged to the Los Angeles club at the time of my visit. For many of them, it is their first step toward exiting the gang life as they enter a new door of hope in Christ.

During a recent visit to the Los Angeles Center, some of the staff members gave me a tour of the neighborhoods surrounding the facility, and my mind flashed back 35 years to my first taste of gang ministry. I was working with the most celebrated Teen Challenge gang convert, Nicky Cruz. Once a week, he and I drove our cars into the dangerous Williamsburg section of Brooklyn, New York, to round up about two dozen members of the "Hell Burner's" gang (we knew we couldn't handle any more than that). I was so new and naive that I didn't have enough sense to realize that if I said or did the wrong thing, it would have only taken one of them to do me harm.

Nicky had gained the gang members' confidence—I was just his sidekick who came along to provide a ride to the Teen Challenge Center in Brooklyn. Once we finally got the gang to the center, we had to take them in the back door through the kitchen so they could put their weapons in a closet and pick them up on the way out (if they still wanted them after the Holy Spirit was done with them).

Once we were all inside the chapel, Nicky poured out his heart to those young men who were so unaccustomed to sitting in a chapel listening to "preaching." Nicky had a way of commanding attention. He remembered what gang life was like, but he was far enough along in his Christian walk that he knew how to deliver the gospel message accurately to those gang members in terms they could understand. He preached and moved among them fearlessly. I noticed that Nicky simply shared with them the same message of God's love that my brother, David, had shared with Nicky only a few years earlier.

Those chapel meetings were miraculous on two counts. First, it was remarkable that the same man who was now preaching to other gang members had been saved and brought out of the gang life himself! Second, it was a miracle that two preacher's kids from a small town in Pennsylvania—David and I—would be working with inner-city gangs in New York, one of the world's largest cities.

I know that in my mind, I never intended to be an urban gang worker! I felt a call to the ministry at the age of 12, but I fully intended to follow my father's footsteps by pastoring a traditional Pentecostal congregation in some small town in Pennsylvania. I planned to work under my father for a time after graduation from Bible school, but two things changed my destiny: my father's sudden death during my second year of Bible school, and David's divine call to minister to the untouched gang population in New York City.

I went home to Scranton for a weekend visit, and my sister, Ruth, and her husband, Don, asked me, "Do you want to go to New York and hear Dave preach at the gang crusade?" I agreed to go, but had I known how that crusade would affect my life, I might have stayed home!

That crusade just "happened" to be the meeting where Nicky Cruz surrendered his heart to Jesus! My brother vividly described the meeting in his book, *The Cross and the Switchblade*, and it was powerfully portrayed in the movie of the same name. As I look back today, nearly 40 years later, I still consider Nicky's conversion to be one of the great conversions of modern times.

I remember the policeman's reaction in Upper Manhattan when Don and Ruth and I asked him where the St. Nicholas Arena was located. David had booked his gang crusade in an old boxing arena because no church would allow such a meeting in their buildings. He felt the gangs would feel less threatened on "neutral turf," and they were all familiar with the arena. The policeman looked us over, raised his eyebrow, and asked, "Are *you* going to the gang crusade?" Then he gave us an incredulous look as if to say, "What are *you* doing in *this neighborhood* going to a *gang crusade*?!" Astounded or not, he pointed us in the right direction and we managed to find a place to park.

The meeting had already begun and a woman was singing something in Spanish when we walked in. We took a seat in the middle of the arena, in the second section. I couldn't help but notice that we were the only "visitors." A small Spanish choir and a few other brave supporters were seated to the left, and right in front of us was a gang! I realized later that these were the "Mau Mau's," the gang led by Nicky Cruz and Israel. Scores of "Chaplains," "Dragons," "GGI's," and other gang members were scattered elsewhere in the seats. I didn't know enough to be scared, but at least I knew I had never seen any evangelistic crusade like that before!

I didn't see my brother, David, until he came out to preach that night. According to David, his message and the response it brought were poor. I still maintain that his message and delivery were anointed. As far as the gang members' response, history has settled that score.

David wrote about that crusade in *The Cross and the Switchblade*:

> *"I couldn't understand what was wrong with my sermon. I'd done everything I could do to make it a good one. I'd spent hours preparing it, and prayed over every line of it. I'd even fasted in the hope that this would strengthen my delivery and my persuasiveness. But I might as well have stood up and read the stock market report. Nothing I said seemed real to these kids; nothing came through to them. I preached for fifteen minutes, and all I could sense was the growing restlessness of the crowd. I had reached the point in my sermon where I quoted Jesus' command to love one another."*[1]

I can still recall that part of the sermon vividly. David had just begun to say that Jesus meant Italians should love Puerto Ricans, and Puerto Ricans should love Italians. Suddenly, one of the gang members about ten rows in front of me stood up and shouted something in Spanish. Now back where I came from, we threw people out of the church for doing something like that, but no one made a move to stop the boy's shouting.

The angry gang member was challenging David's message of love, saying, "I got a bullet hole here, preacher! One of them n- - - -r gangs did it. And you say we're supposed to love them?! Man, you're not real!"

I could tell that David was frustrated and didn't know what to do. He just bowed his head and prayed (while I kept my eyes *wide open*). The next thing I knew, gang members were standing up and leaving their seats! At first, I was sure they were leaving the meeting, but once they reached the aisle, they marched right down to the altar at the front of the stage!

Then the gang right in front of me suddenly stood up! Israel, the president of the "Mau Mau's," had been powerfully touched by the Spirit of God in the midst of all the confusion and restlessness in that place. He nudged Nicky and told the rest of the gang to follow him to "the preacher." He said, "We're going to give our hearts to God," and they did it—in large numbers. Just as the "Mau Mau's" had faithfully followed Israel and Nicky into deadly gang battles and crime, they now followed their leaders to "the preacher." No one realized it at the time (including David and I), but history was in the making.

David later told me, "The conversion that was hardest for me to believe was Nicky's. I'll never forget him standing there with a big grin on his face, saying in his strained and stammering way, 'I'm giving my heart to God, David.' I couldn't believe him because the change seemed too sudden. He was puffing away on his cigarette, and little jets of smoke were streaming out of the sides of his mouth while he told me something new had happened in his heart. What about the narcotic addiction? What about the stealing and mugging, the heavy drinking, the brutal stabbings, and sadism? Nicky must have read my thoughts because he quickly defended himself by using the only technique he knew—cursing: 'Damn it, David! I've given my heart to God!' "

By that time, I had made my way backstage, and the altar workers had completed their ministry to all the gang members who had gone forward. I stood next to Nicky (who didn't know who I was), and I remember being struck by what I thought was his small size, and by the miniature cane he carried everywhere.

The gang members asked for Bibles, saying, "Give us them *big ones*, David, so people can see what we're carrying!" Once they had their Bibles, the gang members disappeared into the night on their way back to their gang turf in Brooklyn. Little did I know as I stood beside that skinny, wiry, olive-skinned gang leader backstage that night, that just a few years later, I would be working with Nicky in a ministry to gangs called "Teen Challenge."

My Pentecostal church upbringing taught me that one must obey God's call—wherever it leads. I'd sung the words many times, "I'll go where You want me to go, dear Lord...I'll be what You want me to be...." I meant every word of it. I was prepared to go over mountains, cross plains, and go overseas, but somehow I never thought inner-city streets were included in that scenario. They never told me God's call might lead me far from Pennsylvania's peaceful towns to the high-rise buildings, mean city streets, and gang turf of New York's youngest gangsters! I had no idea I was being sent to unreached "urban tribes" with names like the "Hell Burners," the "Roman Lords," and the "Ralph Avenue Boys."

Years and decades have gone by, and as I talk to the new generation of Teen Challenge workers, I've discovered that most of them are products of the ministry itself! When I see the fire and passion in their eyes, I can't help but feel the same surge of adrenaline and apprehension I felt when I first drove a carload of what some called "savages" to the original Teen Challenge Center in Brooklyn, New York, to hear about a Savior who died for them!

When my brother, David, took a risk by faith to share the gospel of love with Nicky Cruz and his friends, he accomplished much more than winning some gang members to Christ. He literally brought the saving message of God's love to a whole new unreached people group, just as William Cary and David Livingstone brought the gospel to unreached people in India and Africa respectively more than a century earlier! The big city street gangs of the late 1950's and 60's represented America's most neglected and unreached evangelism frontiers.

These young toughs, with their strange culture of violence and crude street language, were operating right in our "front yard." Nicky's "Mau Mau's," the inner-city gang from the Fort Green ghetto of Brooklyn, may as well have been the violent secret society from Africa called the "Mau Mau's," from which the gang took its name. Now as then, gangs are the "untouchables" of society, and are both feared and neglected by the Church at large. Praise God, He changes impossible situations.

Today, nearly 40 years after David took the first step by preaching to some bored New York City gang members in a boxing arena, new hearts and voices are taking their places beside him with every day and week that passes. Teen Challenge is raising up the cross of Jesus Christ as the only answer to the gang problems faced by Los Angeles, New York, Chicago, Detroit, Houston, and other cities around the world. A strange and exciting trend has emerged over the years that is bringing new life and hope to gang-dominated urban areas. I visited several churches near the Los Angeles County Teen Challenge Center recently. Those churches were built and filled by stable middle-class families at one time, but as the neighborhoods changed, many families moved away. The church congregations slowly dwindled away and died, leaving many church facilities empty, and denominational leaders uncertain about what to do with them. Then Teen Challenge came along with its army of former drug addicts and gang members and a burning vision to reach out to the neighborhoods many now feared and avoided.

I listened to Phil Cookes challenge some volunteer workers who were about to go out into the gang-dominated area surrounding the church he pastors. He knows what he is talking about. Phil ministers to a congregation composed of people from three adjoining communities. Fourteen thousand gang members also live in those communities.

Phil grew up in Los Angeles County, and he committed his first crime at the tender age of five. By the age of seven, he had formed his own "kiddie gang" and was ready to stand up to anybody to defend his turf. He fell deeper and deeper into gang life through his teens. Phil says the gangs provide a sense of security for their members; they share a sense of "belonging" that many don't feel at home. "I liked the image of the gang member," Phil recalls. "To me, it represented manhood—and the kind of warrior I wanted to be. I even had a Mongolian warrior tattooed on my arm."

In his teens, Phil began a decade-long series of trips to the county jail, and he began taking heroin. His dad gave up on him and called him an "outlaw," and by the age of 20, Phil was a full-blown heroin addict. He plunged even deeper into a life of crime to support his "habit." After several years of heroin addiction, Phil realized that he needed help. He was in prison at the time, so he poured over self-help books at the prison library in search of answers, and he sought psychiatric help.

"I did everything I knew to do to change my life," Phil said. "One time when I was up for parole, I made an appointment with one of the prison psychiatrists. He looked at me across his desk and said, 'Philip, you are going to have to stop drinking alcohol.' I answered, 'I know that.' Then he said, 'You're going to have to stop using heroin,' and I answered, 'I know that too.' Then he said, 'You are going to have to stop committing crimes, Philip, if you want to stay out of here.' Then I answered, 'I know all that! But how do I do it?' "

Phil shook his head and continued, "That psychiatrist had *four degrees* hanging on the wall behind him. But do you know what he did? He looked me straight in the eyes and said, 'I'm going to be real honest with you—*I don't know*!' " Fortunately, a friend came to Phil one day and shared Jesus Christ with him. Phil accepted

Christ, but in his unrenewed state, he took a massive dose of heroin just a few days later and almost died. God intervened and spared his life, and in 1983, Phil rededicated his life to the Lord and put 16 years of heroin addiction behind him. One year later, he entered Teen Challenge.

Today, Phil is happily married with two beautiful children—and he is the director of the Los Angeles County Teen Challenge. He is a licensed Assemblies of God minister, and the pastor of the same church in Hawthorne where he was captured in the parking lot by police and arrested at the age of 15! He said he used to sell heroin from a location only two houses away from the church he now pastors!

At another church, I met Keith Jackson, a husky red-haired man in his early 30's. He and his wife, Candy (a former drug addict), returned to the same kind of neighborhood in which he had grown up, and they now pastor the Lynwood Worship Center and aggressively reach out to local gangs. During a tour of the building, I asked Keith where the bathroom was. He just smiled and asked me to follow him. "Let me show you something," he said, as he led me to a window in the bathroom that faced the front street. "A few days ago, a gang fight broke out on the corner. One of the bullets came through the window," he said casually.

Some churches have busy traffic to contend with. Teen Challenge and inner-city churches have to dodge flying bullets. Keith told me a young pregnant mother was fatally shot right in front of the Teen Challenge home in Los Angeles, and her last conscious moments were spent in the arms of a Teen Challenge staff member who told her about Jesus.

One of the more unusual ways Keith reaches out to area gangs is by sponsoring car washes to pay the funeral expenses for slain gang members. After agreeing to help in one of those situations, Keith got a call from a "shot caller" (a gang leader), who told him, "Look, we've had two guys go down in the last month, and each time you let us have a car wash to pay for their funerals. You are all right. We got your back [covered]. Whatever you need us to do for you, you just let us know."

Teen Challenge workers around the world "step into harm's way" every day for the sake of Christ. Robin and Patty, both 20 years old, are Teen Challenge workers at the Los Angeles Center. These two young women left the center one night and were greeted by members of the "Los Padrinos" gang as they hung out across the street from the center. Robin knew every one in the group of seven boys and two girls because they attended some of the weekly meetings at the center.

Patty started talking with Conejo (a Spanish nickname meaning "rabbit"). Conejo was 18, and his heart was hardened toward the gospel. When Patty asked him why he was so hard, he said, "Look. Everybody's got to die sometime! Even you are going to die." Patty knew that having no fear of death was one of the many invisible "badges" that gang members claim to wear.

"You're right, it will happen to all of us," Patty boldly replied. "That's why it's so important to know where we're going after we die—*we have to know we are ready to meet God*. I will die, but I know I have an angel before me, and my life is in God's hand."

Only minutes later, a young man fired more than 11 shots at the group from a distance of only 20 feet! Patty had no place to run since she was near the curb, so she hit the pavement and lay flat. Robin ran with the other youths and vaulted a fence to find shelter behind some buildings, and then the drive-by shooter sped away into the night.

When everyone returned to the attack scene, they found Patty unhurt, but Conejo had been hit three times: once in each leg, and once in the arm. Conejo was rushed to the hospital, and Patty and Robin went along to make sure he was all right. One of the gang members managed to sneak past hospital security to see his wounded friend, and when he returned to the waiting area, he said, "Conejo really wants to see the church lady [Patty]. He wants to talk to her real soon." Patty was finally able to talk frankly with Conejo about eternal things in the Intensive Care Unit. Conejo's hardened heart was opened to the gospel because Patty had trusted God to protect her, and He kept His word during the brush with death she shared with Conejo on that dark night in Los Angeles.

Another shooting occurred only a few weeks later, and this time Robin was struck in the side by a bullet that ricocheted off a wall. She was in a yard filled with neighborhood children when the attack occurred, but she was the only one hurt in the hail of bullets. Thanks to God's protection, her wound was not serious.

In Orange County, California, Teen Challenge holds weekly gang "rallies" to further train and disciple gang members who have been won to Christ in city park ministry, neighborhood street meetings, and personal evangelism. Those who truly want to grow in their commitment to the Lord may attend even more intensive weekly Bible studies. These gang "rallies" provide great potential for good—and for trouble as well.

One night, two rivals from different gangs showed up at the same rally. One had tried unsuccessfully to kill the other recently, and the word on the street was that the "victim" was out for revenge. The gang member who had attempted to murder his rival had just accepted Christ and entered the Teen Challenge resident program. As the two rivals entered the grounds, all the other gang members and the staff watched warily to see what the avenger might try to do. After some tense moments, he made peace with his rival. By the end of the service, he also made peace with God and surrendered his life to Christ! He ended up in the resident program with his former rival, and the two bitter rivals literally worshiped God and "hung out" together, supernaturally united in Christ!

One particular outreach in Orange County especially caught my attention: "God's Gang Youngsters" is an outreach to preteens using special meetings separate from teen meetings. Most of the preteens reached by this ministry are from one-parent homes in gang-dominated areas. If they are not reached for Christ at an early age, it is almost certain they will graduate to become tomorrow's gang members, gang leaders, or drug addicts. The goal of Teen Challenge of Orange County is to "get them before the fact instead of after the act."

The day I visited the Orange County Teen Challenge Center, more than a hundred workers were preparing for a "gospel invasion" of the streets in the area. As the workers went out into the street, a police officer yelled out of his cruiser window to a Teen Challenge student worker, "Got anyone saved yet?" The worker smiled and waved back, and said, "No, not yet. But we just started!" Had the policeman returned later, he could have seen a list of all the new converts' names, and in some cases, he could have looked into their faces.

At one location, two Orange County police officers were about to arrest three drug addicts when they saw some Teen Challenge street outreach workers approaching. They motioned to the workers to come over, and then the officers told the addicts, "If you talk to these guys, we won't arrest you this time." Our workers were able to share the gospel with a "captive" audience!

One of the Orange County volunteers was grazed by a bullet when a gang war suddenly broke out near the outreach area that night. Apparently a bullet from a gang member's gun had ricocheted off a police helicopter and hit the worker! The Teen Challenge volunteers refused to run that night—they had made the commitment to risk their lives if necessary to demonstrate that *the cross is still mightier than the switchblade!*

Endnotes

1. David Wilkerson, *The Cross and the Switchblade* (New York: The Berkley Publishing Group, 1962), p. 78.

Chapter 2

Take Him to the Streets

The tall young Swede defied my idea of his nation's mild-mannered and fair-haired male image. Mikael is definitely blond, but he is far from mild-mannered! Every ounce of his six-foot-three frame pulsates with a love and drive for missions and face-to-face street evangelism.

I met Mikael and members of his team when I spoke at the Sweden Teen Challenge Training Center in Moholm, Sweden. Each year, students are drawn to that center from across Sweden, motivated by a deep desire to reach Sweden's troubled and hurting people in schools, in tent crusades, in coffee houses, and through one-on-one personal evangelism. It was during one of those training meetings that Mikael heard the divine challenge to go to the 60 million Turks who have not been effectively evangelized!

Teen Challenge had received an invitation to send representatives to Izmir, Turkey (the probable site of the first-century city of Smyrna), from a man who said he had a disco club. When he offered Mikael and his team the opportunity to put on a drama in his disco, Mikael jumped at the chance to present Christ in the heart of this ancient Islamic nation.

When Mikael arrived with his team in Turkey to walk through this unique door of opportunity, there was *no door*. "When I got there, the man was gone," Mikael told me. When I asked him what they did, he said, "We prayed!"

I thought to myself, *How could Mikael conduct relationship-based personal evangelism openly on the streets of Turkey, of all places? For one thing, you don't talk to long-term missionaries!*

"Everyone was fearful and intimidated," Mikael said sadly. "I met missionaries who had been working in Turkey for years—with no results whatsoever. There are only about 500 known or open converts to Christianity in all of Turkey, and the largest evangelical church in the whole country only has about 40 to 50 members. It was time to break out of the traditional methods of evangelism in Turkey."

Mikael was not complaining, nor was he being arrogant or prideful about his own efforts to take Jesus to the streets among the Moslems. I asked him, "So the door you thought was 'open' was suddenly 'closed.' What did you do after you prayed?" I had two reasons for questioning Mikael. I knew Turkey was not considered an "open field" to the gospel—many Christians had been put in prison for public witnessing in recent years. I also wanted to find out how the Teen Challenge ministry could be used as an evangelism tool in such a closed Moslem culture.

Mikael described his next move: "I went into one of the largest discos in the city and told the owner about our original plan to do drama in a disco. He actually invited us to do it there! He had a large dance hall. In fact, it was *very large* for that area, since it could hold about 5,000 people."

I could not imagine how the gospel could be shared in such a setting, unless it was through traditional open-air preaching, which I knew was virtually impossible. I didn't have to wait very long to hear Mikael's solution to the problem:

"We do a complete drama with a sound track in the Turkish language. It begins with creation and ends at the cross," Mikael explained. I had to interrupt him and ask, "Are you saying that you can actually get away with preaching about the cross and presenting the gospel of Christ? Aren't you dealing with Moslems?"

My enthusiastic Teen Challenge coworker smiled and explained, "Most of the Turkish people are secular, but even the devoted Moslem has no problem with Jesus. We even give out literature on the streets!" By now I was sitting on the edge of my seat, and I asked, "And you had no trouble?"

"Oh yes, we've had troubles. I was put in jail, threatened, and nearly beaten. We have been thrown out of several places, and the police and security bureau have us under constant surveillance. I discovered that *it is not illegal to preach the gospel in Turkey!* The Holy Spirit urged me to visit the local police commissioner, and I did. Eventually the Lord even gave us favor with the chief of police—I've had coffee with him! Now, whenever we want to go into a new area to evangelize, I tell the police officer ahead of time. That way we don't have problems."

Mikael smiled and said, "One police detective who had had a bit too much 'raki' [Turkish vodka], even admitted to me that the police station had received a lot of calls from people reporting us. Can you imagine the Bible creating chaos like that?" he said, tongue in cheek. "This detective was involved in investigating us once before. He was forced to read the New Testament they had impounded, and he even had to watch the 'Jesus' movie! He said he liked it, but he couldn't understand why Jesus had to be crucified." Mikael grinned and joyfully remarked, "I quickly explained why."

I finally asked, "Have you had any results? Were there conversions?" Then Mikael answered, "When we preach, or share, or give out literature, we get one of two possible results: Either people are open and positive, and accept the message; or they are terribly upset that we have disturbed their slumber on their way to destruction. We have seen both.

"Many people receive us with open arms. Our practical outreach efforts take two forms. We conduct evangelistic 'raids' into discos where we perform drama, preach the gospel, and give out free Bibles. We also arrange open meetings where we show the 'Jesus' movie, share the Word of God, and pray for the sick. God wants to reveal His power in many ways. Healing is a strong proof and evidence to unsaved people that God loves them."

The workers had some surprises along the way. "One man came into one of our meetings with a whole group of men who were all upset," Mikael said. "This man was determined to disrupt our service. When the commotion finally died down, he told us why he was upset—totally unaware that he was literally giving a strong testimony to the crowd!

"He said he had come home from work earlier that day, and one of his children came to him asking, 'Dad, who is this Jesus?' He didn't know how to answer," Mikael said. "His son continued, 'The tourist group [Mikael's Teen Challenge team] always talks about a Jesus who can heal the sick. Dad, you know that Mom has terrible headaches, and when we prayed to Allah, as Mohammed said, nothing happened. Now the tourist group has prayed for her in the name of this 'Jesus.' Dad—Mom is well now! *Who is Jesus?*' "

The man was so furious that he told a group of his friends. "They came in and started screaming, and disrupted our meeting," Mikael recalled. "But in the end, that father unknowingly delivered our strongest testimony of the night!"

Ten healings have been confirmed since they began the work in Turkey. "Several eyes have been opened," he said. "One day, two of our evangelists were witnessing on the beach, and they gave a Bible to a person selling corn-on-the-cob. The man looked at the book and explained that his eyesight was so bad that he couldn't read at all. When one of the evangelists asked if he could pray for the man's eyes, the man said he could.

They prayed for him right there on the beach! Then the man started flipping through the Bible, saying, 'I can see! I can see!' as he read the book. He thanked our workers for the miracle and the Bible, and they explained that *God* had healed him—in the name of Jesus."

In Mikael's latest communication from Turkey, he reported: "Tomorrow is a great day. We will have the first baptismal ever in the history of 'Filippus' Teen Challenge mission in Turkey! For five years, our work and prayers have been centered on ministry here. Now people are starting to be healed and saved. Hallelujah! That figure of only 400 to 500 known converts in Turkey will soon be distant history."

After my conversation with Mikael, I returned to my room to prepare to minister to the Swedish Teen Challenge workers that evening, some of whom were going to Turkey to be part of the Moslem ministry. As I prayed that night, I thanked the Lord for yet another miracle. Somehow, God had carried the love and boldness of a ministry birthed on the front lines of New York's gang turf to Scandinavia, where it had played a role in reaching Moslems for Christ. My thoughts turned to memories of my own beginnings in street evangelism ministry.

Before I began working with Nicky Cruz on the streets to reach New York's gangs, my brother, David, gave me another, less glamorous assignment. It was my first "real job" after finishing my Bible training, and I had just moved to New York to join my brother's fledgling ministry.

David had written some literature for youth, and as he began traveling and sharing his vision for inner-city work, God began to raise up other visionaries. As these people caught the vision for street ministry, they asked David for copies of the literature that they could use in their area of the country. One tract, entitled "Chicken," was especially popular. It was based on a dangerous contest of will popular with teens in the late 50's and 60's, in which two drivers would drive their cars directly toward one another at high speed. The first driver to turn aside to avoid a collision was called "chicken." This tract became an instant hit among the few people who were involved in outreach evangelism in those days.

When David established a New York office for the Teen Challenge ministry (known at first as Teen Age Evangelism), he needed someone to set up a small shipping and mailing department to handle the many requests for the "Chicken" tract and other literature David had written. He found the perfect candidate for the job—me!

At first, I thought the job was very humiliating. I wanted to *go on the streets*, not send literature to others so they could do it. I didn't say anything to my brother about this, but I did grumble to the Lord: "How can You do this to me? I have been preaching since I was 16! You have called me to this great city. I am even an ordained minister. Why am I working in an office mailing out tracts?"

When the situation didn't change, I complained even harder to the Lord. This time I reminded Him about all my credentials, and I added one more thing: "Lord, besides all the other reasons I ought to be on the streets—I'm Dave Wilkerson's brother!" He was not impressed.

The Lord did speak to me, but on His terms. I heard Him say to my inner man: *"I have not called you to the streets. I have not called you to be successful. I have called you to Me. Be faithful in the little things and someday I'll enlarge your responsibilities."*

I accepted that admonition, and vowed never to complain again about such things. My time did finally come to "take Him to the streets." Some of the most exciting and rewarding ministry I have ever experienced took place in open-air evangelism outreach, one-on-one street evangelism, and other types of outreaches through the ministry of Teen Challenge.

Today, there are Teen Challenge coffee houses located worldwide—there are 16 in Portugal alone! In Great Britain, creative Teen Challenge workers are using double-decker buses as "mobile coffee houses" in Wales, Scotland, and England. Workers witness to youths on one level of the bus, while other workers lead people through the "sinner's prayer" on another level! One worker told me, "As soon as we drive the bus up to designated areas each week, kids are waiting for us. At first they were skeptical, but when we went back again and again, we gained their favor. Now they even bring their friends."

Albania was once the most atheistic communist nation in the world, but God changes things! Nicholas and Elizabeth Frosborg of Teen Challenge, Sweden, have opened a coffee house across the street from a high school in Tarana, Albania. Now, for the very first time, young Albanians flock to the coffee house and hear the gospel in word, music, or through personal sharing from 7:30 in the morning until 9:00 at night! The Frosborgs were forced to hire guards to watch the building at night due to break-ins (something that would never have happened under communism—just as there would never have been a Christian coffee house). This coffee house in Albania offers a unique opportunity to encounter youth who may be afraid to enter a church building.

This has been the key to the effectiveness of Teen Challenge around the world—we go to troubled youth *on their turf*, but we *present the gospel on our terms*. We are careful not to be too pushy, and we avoid "turning off" the youth by being too religious—all without hiding the fact that the reason we go on the streets is to lift up the name of Jesus.

Yet another kind of "coffee house" is operated in Prague, in the Czech Republic. Tom and Lois Loften are Teen Challenge workers and Assembly of God missionaries in that ancient city. Faced with the high cost of renting a building or store front in the central city, Tom came up with a creative and inexpensive way to conduct coffee house evangelism—*without a building*!

Tom said that as he and Lois prayed about how to reach Prague's youth when they didn't have the money or budget to rent a place for a traditional coffee house,

"The Lord showed Lois that we should go to them when they are at their weakest, and we are at our strongest!" After further prayer, they laid out a unique strategy to fish for the souls of young people: they would use the *back of their car* to set up a coffee urn—right in the drug center of the city. Tom and Lois felt the best way to follow the Lord's direction was by setting up at *4 o'clock in the morning*—the hour when many of the city's youth come out of the bars and discos that infest the area! The Loftens pray throughout the early part of the night, and then go where the youth have "spent" themselves on drugs, alcohol, sex, and other things. "When the addicts are tired, empty, lonely, and weak, we lift up the name of Jesus in His strength," Tom said.

Open-air street evangelism is another way Teen Challenge successfully reaches out to inner-city areas around the world. This type of ministry involves the use of good music and powerful testimonies. It is important to have good quality music on the streets because kids are sophisticated today when it comes to music. Any testimonies or preaching has to be short and powerful. In foreign countries, Americans who go on the streets are usually limited by language differences. One of our goals is to raise up indigenous witnesses for Christ, but until the foundation is laid, we use mime, drama, and music because they are effective evangelism tools that can cross any language barrier. In every case, however, God has primarily chosen to use the "foolishness of preaching to save them that believe"

(1 Cor. 1:21). It is no surprise to Teen Challenge workers around the world that *street preaching* is still *the* most effective tool on the streets!

Drug addicts who enter our residential discipleship programs after being won to Christ through this kind of street evangelism are often the best prospects for lifelong service to the Lord. A seed of hope and repentance has been planted in them—the seed of God's Word. A second group of solid prospects includes those who get saved, but who are not addicted to drugs. When they step out of a crowd in their own neighborhood, and in front of their friends and neighbors, they have made a bold step that makes them good prospects for the Kingdom of God.

Teen Challenge conducted an outreach in a neighborhood of high-rise apartments, right in front of a public housing building towering more than 20 stories above the street. The street crowds were large, and many more hung out of their apartment windows in the building behind the speaker to listen and watch what was going on. When the speaker invited people to come forward for salvation, many that had been standing on the street came forward for salvation.

One of the Teen Challenge workers suddenly got an idea and shared it with me. I quickly whispered it in the ear of the speaker, and he went to the microphone and said, "All of you who are listening to the meeting in your apartments: If you want to accept Christ, please let us know by turning on and off a light in your apartment" (it was dark at that point). We rejoiced as light after light went off and back on. Then the speaker challenged the people: "If you turned a light on in your apartment because you want the light of Jesus Christ to be turned on in your heart, then *take the next step*! Come down on the street and let us pray for you!" Praise God, several people got on their elevators and came down to publicly confess Christ.

During these street meetings, the power and presence of God pushes back the darkness all around the streets and the street people as nothing else can. A graphic example of God's intervening power happened one night while we were setting up for a meeting in Harlem, Manhattan. For some reason, the electric generator that supplied the power for the sound system was not working. The technicians tried to fix it, but I told them to give up on the generator and plug into the street light, and I showed them how to do it. (I had used street lights for emergency power many times before that.)

As the workers were making the adjustment, a Teen Challenge worker named Willie came up to me. He said, "Brother Don, do you see that fellow standing over there?" I casually looked around to see the man he was talking about. "He's *casing* the place!" Willie warned me. "He's a drug addict who makes his drug money from robbing apartments."

"How do you know?" I asked. Willie, a former addict himself, nodded toward the man and said, "See the pack on his back? He keeps his burglary tools inside that bag. He's looking over all the instruments and equipment we have here. He's trying to figure out how he can rob us."

"Then you keep your eyes on him all the time, Willie," I said, and he did. I also kept watching the man out of the corner of my eye. When one of the technicians had trouble plugging our power into the street light, he called out for a pair of pliers. "Anyone got a pair of pliers?" When no one responded, the would-be burglar and dope addict reached into his backpack of tools, pulled out a pair of pliers, and handed them to the worker! As soon as our technician completed his task, he gratefully gave them back to the man with the backpack.

A few minutes later, the same worker called out, "Anyone got some wire clippers? I need some wire clippers." Again, no one responded; and once again, the "tool man" reached back to pull out a pair of wire clippers and gave them to the worker! Our technician finally finished the hookup and the meeting was ready to go. Evidently the "tool man" realized he couldn't steal our equipment, but he decided to stick around for the whole service. When the altar call was given, he was the first to go forward, and he entered our program!

As I watched this unfold, the Holy Spirit said, "*Do you see what I can do with the devil's tools? I can take them, and save them, to make new music come out of them; just like that drug addict's tools were used to save the street meeting.*" Some of the greatest miracles of salvation and deliverance have taken place during or as a result of a gospel meeting on the streets!

God does another great work in our open-air and personal evangelism efforts on the streets—He changes our workers. Many who join us are not seasoned street workers—they are simply people with a heart for the lost. They have an especially soft heart for the prostitutes, addicts, and other street people they encounter on the streets. Some go out in fear and trembling, but they usually find they don't have as much to fear as they thought! They are nearly always surprised at how the Holy Spirit is able to use them. The fact is that most people just need the right challenge and opportunity for their gifts and love to emerge. We call it, "Taking on a Goliath"! These "Goliath situations" create supernatural "Davids," and teach young "giant killers" to use the supernatural "slingshot" of grace, power, and truth in Jesus' name. Without these pressure situations, they might never have possessed or used these powerful weapons in God.

Chapter 3

The War on Drugs

The year was 1960. David Wilkerson turned to me and said, "Don, let's make a movie on the drug problem to show churches across the country!" Dave wanted to highlight the hopeless condition of drug addicts and enlist the prayers and Christian support for inner-city ministry.

Since we didn't know any better, and no one else had volunteered for the job, Dave and I rented film equipment ourselves. Then we asked Shorty, a drug addict we'd come to know, if we could come to his "shooting gallery" with our camera and capture the whole thing on film. Shorty agreed on one condition: he wanted money to buy the drugs! That put David and I squarely in the middle of a moral dilemma: *Should we give Shorty the money to buy drugs? If we did, would it be right?*

"What do you think, Don?" my brother asked. "We may as well; he's going to rob someone anyway to get it," I suggested. David agreed, so in the end, he gave Shorty the money. He promptly disappeared, leaving us to ponder the decision we'd made. The fact that our meeting with Shorty had taken place inside a little church in the neighborhood didn't help us feel any better about the situation.

Shorty returned within 15 minutes (in that neighborhood, buying drugs is easier than buying a newspaper). We followed him across the street and up endless flights of stairs to the top of an apartment building. Shorty's "shooting gallery" was tucked away in a small space on the top floor, just out of sight in a doorway leading to the rooftop. Shorty had recruited two other dope addicts to join him in his "film debut."

David and I set up our film equipment as the heroin addicts prepared their "works." David was to be the camera man, and I was to hold the lights. When the camera was ready, David gave a signal to Shorty, who started what I quickly perceived was a ritual that was as sacred to the addict as any religious rite. He removed the brownish-white heroin powder from a cellophane bag and dropped it carefully—as if it were gold dust—into a small bottle cap held with a hair pin (addicts call this a "cooker"). Then Shorty used a syringe to draw water out of a soda bottle and put it in the "cooker" with the heroin powder.

Meanwhile, another addict took out a dollar bill and used a razor to cut about an eighth of an inch off the end of the bill. He wrapped the dollar's edge around the needle and used it as a suction device and to help him hold the needle in place over the small "cooker."

Shorty drew the hot liquified heroin into the syringe while another addict wrapped a belt around the muscle of Shorty's upper arm and tightened it as a tourniquet. Shorty pumped his arm until he found a large vein, and pricked the needle into it. He slowly drew blood upward into the syringe where it mixed with the heroin. Then he pressed the top of the syringe and shot the blood and heroin mixture back in the vein of his arm.

My brother watched all of this through the camera lens—and then he fainted! Somehow I caught the camera as it fell out of his grasp, and managed to keep it from crashing down the stairs. Shorty had just finished shooting up, and he glanced casually over at Dave, who was unconscious. Seemingly unconcerned about my brother's prone body, Shorty slowly passed the used needle to the two other addicts, who went through the same ritual until the heroin was in their veins. The whole time I was thinking, *I sure hope David captured the "shooting up" on film.*

The other addicts left as soon as they had finished injecting themselves with heroin. I was left standing over my brother, David, who was still passed out on the stairs. That whole time I had tried holding the camera and the lights at the same time. Meanwhile, several burning questions kept flashing through my mind: *What am I doing here? How do I explain this scene to the police if I have to call them? And why is the founder of Teen Challenge unconscious on a rooftop in a Brooklyn "shooting gallery"?*

I waited and worried about what to do next until David finally regained consciousness (after what seemed to be an eternity of time). "The blood! The blood!" he said in a moan. "I guess I couldn't handle the sight of the blood, Don." The gruesome ritual must have appeared so large through the perspective of the camera lens that it caused David to faint.

As I helped him to his feet, he said, "Air! I need air!" We left the dim surroundings of Shorty's "shooting gallery" and walked out onto the rooftop to discover that it was a bright sunny day. I remember being especially fascinated by the view—it was my first look from a ten-story, high-rise building. I was so awed by the impressive skyline of Manhattan in the background—including the Empire State building, the United Nations building, and the Chrysler building, among others—that I almost forgot my faint-headed brother!

When I finally looked back at him, he was shaking his head. "Don, we have to do something! We have to help these fellows. Let's pray right now and ask the Lord to help us reach them someway, somehow." Then he led us in a brief prayer in the warm sunlight on that Brooklyn rooftop.

Our less-than-professional movie was eventually completed, which we called "Teenage Drug Addiction," but much more than that was accomplished that day. A supernatural burden and vision for a "Center" to help drug addicts also was born. It was at that very moment, at least from my perspective, that the Teen Challenge ministry to drug addicts was birthed in my heart; and I'm positive it was born in Dave's heart.

We didn't simply capture the dilemma and need of drug addicts on film that day—it was deeply imprinted on my mind and heart by the Holy Spirit. God sealed His call on my life then and there. David's original desire for a center to minister to the gangs now became a place for a different kind of troubled youth as well—the "incurable" drug addict.

Many months later, the very first drug addict entered our new program. My brother interviewed and accepted a fellow named Ralphie into the program, and he asked me if I'd drive Ralphie to his apartment to get his clothes. We drove to his neighborhood on South Second Street in the Williamsburg section of Brooklyn, and pulled up in front of Ralphie's apartment. *It was the very same building where we had filmed Shorty and his friends!* I felt a shiver shoot up my spine, and I felt goose bumps rise on my skin. My mind flashed back to our skyline prayer on that Brooklyn rooftop. Perhaps Ralphie was shooting dope inside his apartment at the very moment we prayed...

The answer to David's urgent prayer went far beyond the establishment of the first Teen Challenge Center at 416 Clinton Avenue in Brooklyn. That first center in the United States became the model for many other places of refuge in the U.S. and overseas where drug addicts and substance abusers could come to be "surrounded by love" and set free through the power of God in Christ Jesus.

The greatest challenge we face when we "take Jesus to the streets" is in dealing with the hard cases—the "hopeless" drug addicts. Drug addicts are the modern "lepers" of our day. As in the days when Jesus walked the earth, they are the outcasts of society, the hopeless misfits that are considered unfit for membership or participation in human society.

The ongoing "war on drugs" is the most difficult of all spiritual warfare Teen Challenge must wage to take the gospel to the outcasts, incurables, and untouchables of our day. There are many opinions about the problem, and almost as many approaches to this war. We know this much: *Teen Challenge has found an answer!*

We quickly discovered that the war on drugs would only be won by winning the hearts, minds, will, and soul of the drug abuser. All other attempts are futile in the end. We never *intended* to get involved in this war at the beginning. My brother David was first drawn to the inner city by *gang warfare*, not by the plight of drug addicts. We soon learned how far-reaching this devilish problem of drug addiction could be.

We watched once-active and healthy gang members slide into the abyss of drug addiction, and we wondered and asked, "What, if anything, could we do to help?" The addicts themselves compared drug addiction to "having a monkey on their back." Once it climbed into your life, it was impossible to get off. "Forget it," the neighborhood experts on drugs told us. "Once an addict, always an addict." One non-user told me, "This monkey is a gorilla—there is no cure and no hope for the mainliner. You are best working with the kids before they begin and try and keep them off. You're wasting your time with the heroin user. They'll never change."

At first the drug problem was not a national concern. As long as the "problem" was confined to the inner city, and particularly among the poor and minorities who lived there, most of the nation at large didn't care. My brother and I traveled outside New York City and warned people everywhere we went that the drug problem would one day spread to the suburbs and the middle class, but few believed us. Most people felt pretty secure in their suburban neighborhoods and in small towns.

The late 60's and early 70's changed all that. A youth rebellion spread across the land—and with it came the widespread use of so-called "recreational drugs." First came the use of marijuana. Street dealers and college professors proclaimed it to be harmless and even helpful to the imagination. Parents blindly told themselves, "Oh, it's okay. Marijuana is a soft drug. Our kids won't touch the hard stuff." But they did.

A deadly mix of LSD ("acid"), uppers, downers, speed, and other drugs, was soon popped, snorted, or injected by middle and upper class youths in "pill parties" where caution was thrown to the wind. Hospital emergency rooms across the country began to report countless "hopeless cases" of young victims whose minds had vegetated or whose hearts had suddenly stopped under lethal avalanches of deadly chemicals.

Suddenly, the country got concerned. Federal tax dollars began flowing for programs to "cure" the addict and stop the drugs. The big question was, *and still is,* "How?" How can a drug addict be cured? Many groups of "professionals" have had their try at it and failed.

Doctors and the organized medical profession were the first to nobly try solving drug addiction. Hospitals instituted new "detox" programs, hoping to cure addicts by "weaning" them from drugs gradually to cleanse the physical body of its poisons over a ten-day or two-week period. Of course it didn't work then, and still doesn't today. Any addict knows that addiction is first a psychological problem, then a physical one.

Then the great social engineers of American society, the sociologists, came up with their analysis of the drug problem. They wisely said, "Let's find out why kids take drugs, and get to the root problem." They seemed to come up with answers very easily. "It's poverty that breeds addiction," some contended. As a result of these "scientific" sociological findings, the "Great Society" government programs of the past were instituted in part to fight crime, drugs, delinquency, and other related problems. The idea was deceptively simple: Give people a better social environment, better education, and better job opportunities. As a result, dependence on other economic "programs" and levels of substance abuse will be greatly diminished. Nearly four decades and billions of dollars later, poverty, drugs, and crime have not only "escaped" untouched, they have exploded to new levels of growth!

The truth is that the "root causes" of these problems cannot be cured with dollars. "If drug use and abuse is supposedly caused by poverty, then why is it growing fastest among rich kids, educated youth, and people from middle and upper class families?" I asked myself.

Poverty is not just economic. There is poverty of the spirit and the emotions that can paralyze a family for many generations. Many parents get so caught up "living the good life" that they neglect their children.

The "head doctors" were the next up to the plate. Eminent psychologists, psychiatrists, and therapists all took their turn to help the substance abuser. Suddenly a whole new crop of "group therapy" and private or individual therapy programs blossomed in our nation's hospitals, prisons, and private treatment centers. Their task was to take the addicted individual "down the back roads of the mind and memory" in search of anything that might have triggered drug use in the first place. The theory behind this is that if you know *why* you took drugs to begin with, and if you deal with it or overcome that issue, then you have removed the reason for your need for drugs.

Again, only minimal success was achieved through the therapeutic approach to drug treatment. Only a highly motivated person would commit to this course of treatment in the first place; and secondly, the best therapy programs are very costly. Worst of all, *analysis without answers* to an individual's spiritual emptiness often raises hopes that can never be realized.

One addict went through 30 days of rigorous private and group therapy, but he went back to drugs the very day he left one of America's finest hospital treatment programs. Why? He later told me, "Reverend, the psychologist told me about the problems I had (during our sessions) that I never knew I had. So, when I left treatment I had all the problems I knew I had before going into the program, plus I came out of treatment with all the *new things* he'd uncovered. The way I see it, I ended up with twice as many problems as when I went in, but I still had no answers."

In the end, this man came to Teen Challenge. He said it only made sense. "I've tried everything else for a cure—I may as well try God." Since God is not enlisted in this war on drugs, the government and the American public are committed to using only secular methods to control the drug problem.

Perhaps the greatest effort made in the "war on drugs" over the past 20 years has been the use of law enforcement agencies to find and intercept drugs at their points of origin. At different times during the various presidential administrations, new emphases have been made to dry up the supply of drugs at their source—even if that source was the poppy and cocaine fields of Asia and Central and South America. President Nixon tried to persuade poppy growers in Asia to plant other cash crops. It worked for a while, until new sources popped up in South America.

I have long advocated the use of the armed forces and the Pentagon's resources in the war against drugs. The Bush administration finally appointed a "drug czar" named William Bennett who believed the same thing. Unlike other government officials and cabinet directors before him, Bennett was at least able to put a small dent in the drug traffic invading our shores.

I still believe every effort should be made by federal and local law enforcement agencies to hit drug sellers and pushers where it counts. They need to quickly arrest and prosecute drug suppliers, middle men, and their street pushers at every opportunity. Unfortunately, the financial commitment to do this with the intensity it takes is just not there, not anymore.

Now there is a new cry in the land—fill the prisons with street criminals, most of whom are *drug addicts*. A *USA Today* report dated August 10, 1995, said the United States prison population hit a new high of 1,055,738 in 1994. Ninety percent of the prisoners who are on drugs go back to them soon as they're released, and many non-users get addicted in prison because so many drugs get smuggled inside!

Drugs and crime are twin siblings afflicting our society. Over the past three decades, your chances of becoming a crime victim increased 280 percent, and your chances of being of victim of *violent* crime increased 469 percent! The unknown and often hidden factor of crime is drugs.

Drugs are deadly in other ways too. Sad experience and the science of statistics have proven that *teenagers using drugs are at least three times more likely to attempt suicide* than teens who do not use drugs! This nation has never faced a problem that has so baffled and defied the private and public sector.

Some loudly claim we should "legalize it." Unfortunately, the historical pattern of secular human societies is that when they can't control their vices, they generally end up legalizing it. This was the case with alcohol and gambling in the U.S., and in other countries, with prostitution.

Alaska decriminalized marijuana, and not surprisingly, the percentage of high school students using dope in Alaska is much higher than the rest of the nation! William Bennett noted that in 1975, Italy liberalized its drug laws "and now has one of the highest heroin-related death rates in Western Europe."[1]

Teen Challenge encountered the drug problem long before these arguments even began. No one really knew how drugs could literally change our youth culture and add another addiction to the epidemic problem of alcoholism. My brother and I were fortunate that we didn't know how bad drug addiction really was—ignorance sometimes is bliss. All we knew was that something, somehow, had to be done!

We saw the drug problem in human terms. Young men growing up in gangs in those days could outgrow them. But when drugs became their focus, they were trapped in a habit they would never outgrow. With very few exceptions, once these young men started down the road of drug use, they inevitably turned into drug abusers. We soon learned that most abusers became hopeless addicts!

Although we foresaw the spread of hard-core addiction and heroin use to other segments of society—no one really believed that housewives, mothers, working class men, and even business executives would be sticking needles in their arms over the lunch hour to inject an illegal "designer-form" of heroin into their bloodstream! I was in the middle of writing this chapter when I had to take my car for service to a local garage. While I was stuck in the repair shop, a television set in the waiting area was tuned to a daytime talk show. Four women were featured—they were all heroin addicts who were trying to stay off the stuff through a recovery program. Two had been normal housewives; another was a nurses' assistant in a hospital emergency ward and a teacher's assistant in a public school (she was a "user" on both jobs); and the fourth had been a working single woman who "copped" her drugs in her local supermarket, among other places! All had been mainline heroin addicts.

One white housewife said she bought her drugs in a black neighborhood. When the talk show host asked, "How did you manage that?" she told him, "Everyone assumed I was a social worker. No one suspects a white woman to be buying heroin." And "buy" she did—up to $100 a day! "Where did the money come from?" a member of the TV audience asked. The mother of six children said, "When you are middle class, you beg, borrow, and do whatever you can to get the money. But pretty soon you lose a lot of friends."

The evidence is clear: Heroin is back. In the 1980's, cocaine was the drug of choice; but in the 90's, heroin is increasingly becoming the preferred drug of choice! Don't think it is just the inner-city youth and adults who are drilling their veins with this stuff. Your nurse in the hospital may be doing mainlining; or the secretary in your office. Just hope and pray your bus driver, cab driver, or commercial jet pilot isn't "using."

A *USA Today* cover story dated August 16, 1995, said, "Heroin, the scourge of the '60's and '70's, is back. But there's something very different about this new epidemic. The drug is so prevalent, so potent, and so cheap, that it has risen from the streets and the opulent underground, and is now invading the living rooms of the middle class."[2]

The article went on to say that the Drug Enforcement Agency estimates that 600,000 "hard-core heroin addicts" now exist in the U.S. The DEA also reports that world production of opium—from which heroin is derived—has *quadrupled* in the past decade. Whereas heroin used to be 4 to 7 percent pure before; today, the average street potency is 40 percent! In fact, some "speciality" heroin is 70 percent pure.[3]

Drug use overall appears to have gone down in the early 90's, but the number of users and abusers is still shockingly high. In the 50's, less than 5 percent of America's youth experimented with illicit drugs before entering tenth grade. By the 90's, 30 percent had done so.

The National Institute on Drug Abuse estimated that 4 million Americans use illegal drugs more than 200 times per year, and 38 percent of all adults admit to having used drugs at least once. Almost 1 in 6 high school seniors has tried cocaine or crack. Meanwhile, the number of current drug users is estimated to be over 13 million![4]

The problem is not limited to the United States. In Switzerland, where addicts are allowed to shoot drugs in a downtown park in Zurich (I have witnessed it), some 700 to 1,000 young adults converge to inject heroin (free needles are distributed by the city). In spite of this "tolerance," Zurich police blame the quest for heroin (which is five times more expensive in Switzerland than in France or Germany) for 500 purse snatchings,

400 muggings, and 3,500 burglaries in 1989 alone! That is a high price to pay for legalizing a killer.[5]

No drug has recently hit the American scene with such stunning impact as "crack," a form of cocaine. Dr. Bennett said when this hit, "we were like a boxer knocked back against the ropes. We lost our balance. Our legs buckled."[6] The effect on crime is devastating, especially in major cities. Just when there seemed to be some encouraging figures relative to drug abuse, along came the latest drug craze, called "crank." Methamphetamine, also called "crystal" and "crank," has been around for years, but its popularity appears to be growing as the top choice of Americans buzzing in life's fast lane. According to the Drug Enforcement Agency, the DEA seized enough methamphetamine to make about 25 million doses—up from 10 million in 1992.[7]

A Scripps Howard News Service article dated July 9, 1995, claimed that *crank*, a "made-in-the-USA" drug, has replaced imported cocaine as the drug of choice among young people in California.

"Crank" appears to be a substitute for heroin, and since it doesn't have the bad rap heroin does, young people are easily fooled into thinking it is less dangerous. According to Mike Herald, a DEA agent from San Francisco, "[*crank*]...is very deceptive and extremely dangerous. At first it gives a sense of euphoria and being more aware, but then a weekend user gets a habit that builds up and the person becomes agitated, nervous, and paranoid. Mood swings lead to depression and violent behavior in some people. Long-term use can induce a state of psychosis."[8] When Eric Smith tossed his 14-year-old son's head out of his van window onto a New Mexico highway, he thought he was disposing of a demon. Smith's grisly act was just another bizarre outburst blamed on methamphetamine.

Deaths from "crank" are up 225 percent in Los Angeles, and 510 percent in Phoenix. "Crank" is "...an unprecedented threat to public safety," according to Arizona Governor Fyfe Symington, who declared war on "meth." He calls it "the most lethal substance to hit the streets in the 35-year war between America and drugs."[9]

The federal government described the magnitude of America's drug problem in its 1996 budget projection:

"Drug abuse and drug-related crime costs the U.S. an estimated $67 billion a year and destroys the lives of our most precious resource—our youth. Illicit drug trafficking breeds crime and corruption across the globe, drug use helps spread AIDS and other deadly diseases, and drug addiction erodes our Nation's productivity. Many of our communities are most acutely affected by drugs and drug-related crime. On many streets, drug dealers control their 'turf,' making law-abiding citizens prisoners in their own homes."[10]

The "war on drugs" obviously has a long way to go. Even the prophetic insight of my brother, David, failed to foresee the size of the drug problem we would have 35 or more years up the road! It was bad enough we first saw it on New York City's mean streets in the 60's.

Today, however, it is not good enough for us to just "curse the darkness"—we desperately need to light a candle!

When my brother got his first glimpse of what I call the "double trouble" of gangs *and* drugs, he had a dream in which he asked himself, "Suppose you were to be granted a wish for these kids. What would be the one best thing you could hope for?" He told me, "I knew the answer: that they could begin life all over again, with the fresh and innocent personalities of new-born children. And more: that this time, as they were growing up, they could be surrounded by love instead of by hate and fear."

He dismissed his dream, thinking, "Of course it is impossible. How can people who are already in their teens erase all that has gone before? How could a new environment be made for them? Is this a dream You have put into my heart, Lord, or am I just weaving a fantasy for myself?"

The answer was strong and urgent: "*They've got to start over again, and they've got to be surrounded by love!*" David said something happened then. "The idea came to mind as a complete thought, as clearly as the first order I received to go to New York! Along with it something else came into my mind—the picture of a house all their own, where these teens could be welcomed—welcomed and loved. They could live in their house anytime they wanted to. The door would always be open; there would always be lots and lots of beds, and clothes to wear, and a great big kitchen!"

When Dave shared his dream with me in 1960, all I could do was say out loud, "Oh, Lord! What a wonderful dream this is! But it will take a miracle, a whole series of miracles such as I've never seen!"

Endnotes

1. William Bennett, *The De-Valuing of America*, "A Touchstone Book" (New York: Simon & Schuster, 1992), p. 117.

2. Karen Thomas, "Heroin Returns as an Upscale Drug of Choice," *USA Today* (August 16, 1995), p. 1.

3. Thomas, "Heroin Returns," p. 2.

4. *Research Almanac* (Julian, California: Julian Press).

5. *World Press Review* (October, 1990), p. 46.

6. Bennett, *De-Valuing*, p. 123.

7. *USA Today* (August 16, 1995), p. 2.

8. *USA Today* (August 16, 1995), p. 2.

9. *USA Today* (August 16, 1995), p. 2.

10. U.S. Government 1996 Budget Projections, May 18, 1993 (Congressional Research Service).

Chapter 4

Surrounded by Love

In 1960, on a quiet street in Brooklyn, David's dream of a home where troubled youth could come and be "surrounded by love" came to pass. I ran that home and the Teen Challenge Center in New York City for nearly 27 years.

Shortly after the first Teen Challenge resident's home opened, it became the prototype for other Teen Challenge homes in other major cities across the United States. Today, more than 120 Teen Challenge Center resident homes surround teens in love to *make a difference* for Christ in their lives and communities. On any given day of the week, worldwide, more than 3,500 young people, ranging in ages between 16 and 40 (some are even older in a few cases), are "surrounded by love" according to the pattern laid down in my brother's dream more than 40 years ago!

David's dream quickly spread overseas to Holland, Great Britain, Germany, Denmark, Portugal, Guatemala, Costa Rico, Paraguay, India, Australia, Canada, and many other countries (nearly 50 countries across the world currently host Teen Challenge ministries in one form or another). Teenagers and adult men and women of all races, cultures, classes, and religions are finding *the Answer* to drugs and alcohol, and other life-controlling problems through the gospel of Jesus Christ and the work of Teen Challenge.

When these people leave their Teen Challenge resident home after approximately a year, far more will succeed and "stay clean" for the *rest of their lives* than those who will fall back! In 1994 alone, nearly 1,800 students graduated from our Teen Challenge Centers worldwide! Nearly all of these individuals came to us in a severely addicted state that most laypeople and professionals alike would label as "incurable and hopeless."

Why does Teen Challenge work?

The answer is simple and yet profound at the same time. *When there is no demand for drugs*, business will dry up because there will be no "takers." If you really want to eliminate the source of supply for something, then eliminate *the need* for it. The answer and cure for drug addiction begins in the mind, heart, and will of the drug user. If the craving is gone—the pusher loses his power and disappears. Once an individual has the power to say "no," the tempter has no customer. Most of our nation's efforts and resources were spent vainly trying to "solve" the drug problem by "drying up the source of supply." This may have put a small dent in the drug traffic for a short time, but in the end, one fact remained: "As long as there is a market for drugs, there will be sellers."

How can the incredibly addictive power of drugs over minds, bodies, and souls be broken? The only answer to the power of drugs is a "Higher Power." Teen Challenge clearly and boldly declares *who* this "Higher Power" is: Jesus Christ, the Son of God.

Our philosophy and program are based totally on the belief that a person's behavior can only be permanently changed by changing the individual's heart and thought processes. This is done by applying proven, positive, biblical principles leading to a personal and supernatural conversion experience. Deliverance and life-long freedom from addiction can only come through a personal relationship with Jesus Christ.

Unlike the countless secular treatment theories and programs, the Teen Challenge program deals with the *whole person*—physical, mental, emotional, and *spiritual.* Good work habits, good behavior patterns, and strong character are the natural and inevitable results of the in-depth Bible teaching and Christian atmosphere that extends over the year-long live-in program. From the very beginning, we based the cure to addiction on this Bible truth: "Therefore if any man be in Christ, he is a new creature: old things are passed away; behold, all things are become new" (2 Cor. 5:17).

Jesus Christ can transform *anyone* into a "new creature," and force the failures and shame of the past to "pass away." Drug addicts are driven and broken by their chemical bondage. They not only need salvation for their soul, they also desperately need what only Jesus Christ can give them—the creation of a new mind to fight the drug temptation, the re-creation of their battered emotions to deal with the emotional damage of broken relationships, and the healing of a spirit that died as a result of sin.

The first step to true salvation, with genuine deliverance from addiction, is to *place blame where it belongs*. The addict must realize and accept the fact they he or she is *responsible for his or her own downfall*. That downfall began when God was rejected or ignored. The Psalms graphically describe the condition of the substance abuser: "Hungry and thirsty, their soul fainted in them …[who] rebelled against the words of God, and contemned the counsel of the most High" (Ps. 107:5,11).

This rebellion is called sin, and sin separates man from God. The drug addict is *not* a sinner because of drug use. Drug use is, first of all, the *result* of sin. We're born into it. "There is none righteous, no, not one" (Rom. 3:10b).

Repentance, the process of *turning away* from sin, is what opens the way back to God. Drug addicts (and *all sinners* for that matter) must see themselves as sinners who need to repent and turn to God. Otherwise they will never find the mercy and grace God has for them, and they will never enjoy a personal relationship with Jesus Christ. Jesus drew a line and made it clear: "…I am the way, the truth, and the life: no man cometh unto the Father, *but by Me*" (Jn. 14:6).

During a meeting with officials on the island of Barbados about their drug problem, Jerry Nance, of Florida Teen Challenge, and I told the officials about Teen

Challenge. When they asked, "What do you do if the addict is of another religion?" (we knew they were referring to Moslems), I said, "We don't change a person's *religion*. We help change their *lives*. If a drug addict comes to us calling himself a Moslem, a Jew, a Christian, or anything else—we assume his 'religion' *didn't work*, or he would not be an addict! We simply give them a belief and a faith they never had before."

It is hard to explain in non-biblical terms the biblical teaching that sin lies at the root of all man's problems—especially drug abuse. Drug abuse and addiction are moral problems *first*, before they are anything else. When I explained this to one non-addict, he kept comparing himself to drug addicts, and in his thinking, he came off as a pretty good guy. He told me, "I live a good life. I don't really hurt people, and I treat everyone nice, yet you say I'm a sinner! What did I do wrong?"

I just smiled and said, "You were born!" The Bible says, "For all have sinned, and come short of the glory of God" (Rom. 3:23). "Oh, no!" He shot back at me. "No one is born evil! We're *taught* evil by others. Man is basically good. He only does bad things when he is influenced by others and his environment." He had a nice theory, but it was contrary to the Scriptures, and it was *impractical*!

"Do you have children?" I asked. "No," he answered. "Why do you ask?" I smiled and said, "Just wait! Just wait till you have snotty nosed kids running around, and you'll change your mind about original sin. Have you ever watched a child develop his first words? What is the second word they learn to say after 'Mama'? It's usually 'no.' If you ask the child to do one thing, he wants to do something else. Did the child's mother teach him that? No! It's in the child's nature. It's called *self will*—and self is rebellious by nature because our first parents, Adam and Eve, passed that down to us."

That young man went away thinking about what I'd said, but he wasn't ready to admit he was a sinner yet. In some respects, addicts have an advantage over non-addicts—*at least they know they're doing something wrong,* even if they are not willing to change!

This is the teaching that starts addicts on the road to recovery—they must take personal responsibility for their own failure and fall. They must admit that sin is the reason they went astray. Above all, we tell them: *"Quit blaming others."*

Does this mean that we ignore the hurts that other people have inflicted on these addicts? Not at all! We realize mitigating factors often inflict pain and suffering on drug abusers long before they ever turned to drugs. Many of the addicts who come through our doors are victims of parental neglect, physical and sexual abuse, broken homes, angry and abusive fathers, and chronic alcoholism. Many of them grew up in a drug-infested environment, and these are just a few of many factors that can sow the seeds of compulsive drug use, abuse, and ultimate addiction. These harsh realities cannot be ignored. However, once a person is addicted, the only thing that can be done about the past is to find a new *present,* and new hope for the future.

In the Teen Challenge environment, we never allow anyone to "cop a plea" by blaming parents, society, or some other psychological or emotional cause. The "blame game" is not allowed on God's turf.

The bottom line of addiction and alcoholism is that the abuser has chosen to respond to his pain by escaping through drugs. I've seen siblings and neighborhood friends grow up side by side in the same environment, and in some cases, in the same home! Yet, one would turn to drugs or alcohol and the other wouldn't. In fact, many brothers and sisters of drug addicts and substance abusers have become very successful.

People are often surprised to learn that many drug addicts come from good homes, where both parents loved and cared for them. The problems came when these young people chose rebellion rather than a clean lifestyle. For some, their downfall all came down to a single act of curiosity under the pressure of a friend or group of friends who introduced them to drugs. One thing led to another. Don't believe the wishful thinkers—when it comes to any and all types of drugs (marijuana included)—drug *use* nearly always leads to drug *abuse*. Drug abuse turns quickly to *addiction*. Most users will tell you they never *intended* to go as far as they did. When they finally cross the line of no return, it can usually be traced to either the nature of the drug causing the addiction, or the nature of the user—or a combination of both.

It all comes down to a matter of choice. We choose "life or death." Someone has said, "We make our choices, then our choices turn around and make us." How true it is, for better or worse.

The first step toward a new life is to *admit you have a problem*! No one can help an addict who is into denial. The most difficult situations for spouses, parents, family, and friends, are those times when they are trying to help a loved one who does not want to be helped. When parents have tried to pressure their sons or daughters to go into Teen Challenge, their efforts nearly always fail. These unwilling "recruits" must often be turned away until they want to change. It is a sad fact that *some people have to get worse before they want to get better.*

How does change come about? Once people admit they have a problem, it is equally important for them to know *what* their problem is. Diagnosis is as important as the "prescription for the cure." For too long, the treatment of addiction has dealt exclusively with the effects of drugs, rather than the cause. The natural result was that even the cause of drug addiction was often consistently misdiagnosed.

Society has sought for years now to get to the root of the addiction problem. Teen Challenge makes it simple for the addict. The Bible makes it clear: *Sin is the root—addiction is the fruit.* New fruit cannot grow until there are new roots.

The second step for drug addicts seeking a new life is for them to meet the one Person who has the only positive, lifetime cure for their pain. We call this step the "Total Cure of the Total Person." It can only be taken after a person is ready to admit his problem and acknowledge and confess that sin is its source. At this point, we ask him, "Do you want *Jesus* to be your cure?"

The "cure" Christ offers involves the whole man. He transforms the whole person, beginning with a *spiritual* transformation. Then the cure moves on to include the renewal of the mind, the healing of the emotions, and even the restoration of broken relationships.

Prayer becomes the key that opens the way to God through His Son, but God's miracle-working power is only activated by a voluntary, desperate cry for help. For this reason, we are especially careful not to coerce, manipulate, or pressure a person in any way to accept Christ. This act must be a personal and individual decision. This decision sometimes takes place on the street or in an outreach meeting before the addict enters our doors. This sure makes it easier to work with them. The reality is that most have not made that decision yet when they come to us.

The hardest decision many drug addicts ever make is the decision to seek help in the first place. Once an addict enters the Teen Challenge program, the new resident is given many opportunities to call on God and surrender to Christ. Some never make this decision, and leave the center voluntarily—and most residents take days or even weeks before they make the decision to turn their lives over completely to God. Residents who have not made that decision are allowed to stay as long as they abide by the rules. We recognize and honor the fact that, ultimately, salvation must be a work of the Holy Spirit, which causes the sinner to make the decision freely.

It isn't easy to sit by and watch the residents who have not yielded to God—while leaving them alone. Knowing the dangers they will face if they leave Teen Challenge without being changed, I sometimes feel an urgency to "push them" a little toward the Lord. I used to give in to my urge, but when the Holy Spirit rebuked me for it, I quickly stopped interfering in His work.

Before I was "reprimanded" by the Lord, I had a habit of moving the "back seaters" forward in the Teen Challenge chapel services. I knew that many of these "back seaters" were rebels and indifferent people who had come to Teen Challenge because there was nowhere else to go; or because they needed "three hot's and a cot" (three good free meals, and a bed to sleep on). They figured even Teen Challenge, though it was a religious program, was better than prison or the streets. Their hearts and minds had not been captured, and they had erected barriers to the preaching and counseling.

My "brilliant plan" put them right up front, where I could "work on them" during the service. And they were surrounded by the "saved" residents who sang with gusto, prayed loud, and always jumped up when given an opportunity to give a personal testimony of their faith.

I thought my idea was pretty good, but one time, as I once again said, "Come on, fellows, move up!" I felt the Holy Spirit say to my inner man, "Don't do that anymore—because *where they sit is where they're at.*" I knew this was a message from the Holy Ghost, but I wasn't sure what it meant. I quietly breathed a prayer. "Lord, will You run that by me again?" He once again said, *"Where they sit is where they're at!"*

I finally understood that where the men had chosen to sit in the chapel was an outward sign of what was going on in their hearts! The people up front were the seekers. They wanted to be close to the preacher to hear the Word, and close to the altar when it was time to pray. Those in the middle were also "in the middle" spiritually. They were the "fence-sitters" who had not made up their minds to serve the Lord. Those in the back seats either felt far from God, or they wanted to keep their distance. When I finally saw this powerful, illustrated sermon before my eyes, I quietly told the Lord, "Yes, You are right. Where they sit is where they're at with You, Lord." Then I felt the Holy Spirit also say, "You can't move them toward Me, but My Spirit can!"

I have seen the Holy Spirit work impossible miracles over the past four decades! I've seen Him move on the most hardened hearts as the message of salvation was given. When desperate people reach out in faith for His forgiveness and delivering power, they almost always show immediate changes in their attitude, outlook, and behavior. In the very next service, these "hardened" residents will often automatically move toward the front of the chapel. I call it the "Holy Ghost push." It is far more effective than the best human interference.

At one time, I was puzzled about why some Teen Challenge residents are so quick to respond to the message of salvation. They seem to find instantaneous deliverance, while most residents do not! I finally discovered that most of the residents who respond so quickly and powerfully have praying parents, grandparents, or a relative who has been faithfully believing God for their salvation and healing. If you are praying for a troubled child or relative, *never, ever give up*! I know. I've seen the results of those prayers too many times to doubt their power!

Another group of addicts who have readily accepted the Lord are those who heard about Jesus Christ from a friend. When a drug user is told about the saving power of Christ from a *former addict*, the testimony is a powerful example to those still in bondage.

One converted addict returned to his neighborhood and ran into a group of old addict friends. They gave him the "once over" and mocked him, saying, "You'll never last!" Another friend laughed and said, "You just traded one addiction for another." Another friend taunted him, "Come on, Jose—I got some stuff right now. You want some?"

Jose walked away discouraged. He wanted so badly to witness to them, but now he had been "laughed off the street." He walked away as fast as he could, but a half block away, one of his old friends ran up behind him. "Jose, Jose, wait! I want to talk to you."

Jose turned around and looked into the face of one of his ridiculers. "Listen, Jose. We set you up, man! We saw you coming and agreed we'd have a little fun with you. But man—we were just testing you. We figured if you were phony, you'd break down and maybe even shoot up with us. But you didn't! Now we know what you have is *real*. Keep following your new way of life, *'cause if you can make it, it means we can make it* when we're ready!"

Jose walked away rejoicing that he had been a faithful witness. He had also learned something that all must learn if they want to reach out to people with life-controlling problems: They must be "ready" and willing to change. Jose had genuinely turned away from drugs in his heart. Many do not. Some people are not sick enough of their lifestyle to seek help. Help can only come when or if the pain of addiction becomes greater than the pleasure of the addiction.

Teen Challenge only admits residents into its program who want a *new life*. We're not out to simply get rid of the *effects* that lifestyle has brought—we are determined to lay the axe of God to the *root* of the problem! Many people are sorry that they "got caught," or that their addiction has ruined their lives. This kind of so-called "sorrow" creates personal problems. The rebirth of the spirit requires "godly sorrow." The Bible says, "Godly sorrow brings repentance that leads to salvation and leaves no regret, but worldly sorrow brings death" (2 Cor. 7:10 NIV). Worldly sorrow accomplishes nothing. This is why the only approach to the drug and alcohol problem that *really works* is the Christ-centered spiritual approach based on the teachings of the Bible.

The truth can hurt, and the cure for addiction and sin usually involves pain. When people admit to their own sin, and accept personal responsibility for the bad choices that led them down the road to addiction, they will feel pain and sorrow. When they admit that their own sin has created havoc in their relationships with spouses and family, it is vitally important that they be "surrounded by love" in a safe, caring environment such as the Teen Challenge Center. True healing flourishes in residents who know that no matter what they've done, that no matter how bad they've been, God loves them. We tell all of our residents the good news from God's Word that liberates: "...while we were yet sinners, Christ died for us" (Rom. 5:8).

It is almost hard for me to believe that over the past 40 years, thousands or perhaps tens of thousands of troubled youth and adults have entered Teen Challenge Centers across the world. They were "surrounded by love" and given a fresh chance to find new hope, and a new future by the goodness of the Lord! My brother's original goal, as described in his book, *The Cross and the Switchblade*, has come to pass! He continues to tell Teen Challenge workers, "If we really meet human need, the world will beat a path to our door."[1]

Dave had no idea how heavily that path to the doors of Teen Challenge Centers would be trodden—or who would unexpectedly show up to see what was going on inside. Nor did he know that, at times, some would even try to stop what was going on.

Endnotes

1. Wilkerson, *The Cross and the Switchblade*.

Chapter 5

The Therapy of Praise

When we opened the first Teen Challenge Center at 416 Clinton Avenue in Brooklyn (where it still operates successfully today), we had some problems and received a lot of complaints from our neighbors. Since then, we have encountered this almost anywhere in the world we have tried to purchase or rent a building in a residential area. Everyone wants something done about the drug problem—but not in *their* neighborhood!

Our neighbors most often complained about the "loud noise" from the chapel. The sounds of joyous praise, worship, and unrestrained prayer could be heard in nearby apartment houses. Since we could not afford air conditioning at the time, the windows had to remain open on hot days. That meant that, like it or not, our neighbors were privileged to be unwilling participants in our services!

The "national anthem" of our center back then was, "There Is Power in the Blood," or as it is sung in Spanish, "Hay Poder, Hay Poder, sin Igual Poder." I'm sure some of the neighbors must have had that tune and every word of every verse rolling around in their heads in *both languages* at night. One thing that hasn't changed with time or faces is the fact that the fellows love to sing and worship!

Another thing that hasn't changed is that our zealous singing and worship wasn't always appreciated as much outside our walls! Someone kept calling the police, who would politely come to our door and ask if we could keep the noise level down. We really tried to comply, but we weren't always successful.

I am convinced that many converted drug addicts think God is deaf! Again and again, I tried to calm down the guys in our chapel services. I even tried to teach them that you don't have to scream at God to be heard! I also taught them that God is not nervous, and that He accepts all kinds of praise and prayers, whether they are loud or soft. My efforts didn't always work.

On one occasion, the Spirit was apparently moving in a very powerful way, and as is often the case with new converts responding emotionally in such an atmosphere, the "noise level" was at a higher decibel level than usual. An angry neighbor called the police and demanded that "the noise be stopped."

Evidently the call came to a desk sergeant at the local police precinct who had handled some earlier complaints about our noisy activities. He decided he would solve "the problem" himself! He quickly piled into a police car and headed for the Teen Challenge Center. Within minutes, he and another officer came barging in the door and stood outside the chapel in the foyer.

"Who's in charge?!" he demanded, as we met in the foyer. Our house supervisor stepped up and said, "I am."

"Listen, we appreciate what you're doing, but that noise in there has got to stop! We've had too many complaints," the sergeant said, visibly upset. "Now go in there and stop that right now!" he demanded.

"It will be over soon, officer," it was explained. "No—stop it right now!" the officer again demanded. The Teen Challenge house supervisor answered, "I can't do that! You see, those are all former drug and alcohol abusers in there." In an effort to reason with the officer, the worker continued, "They're praying and seeking God. That is their group therapy!"

By this time, the sergeant didn't want to hear any explanation. "Okay, then. I'll go in and stop it!" The police sergeant hitched up his gun belt, opened the chapel door, and looked all around inside. He saw some of the men crying, some with their hands raised praising God, and others on their knees. If you've ever been in a Spirit-filled charismatic service, you know what the policemen witnessed. At that time, we were in the midst of a very special outpouring of the Holy Spirit.

The officer stood in the doorway, taking in the whole scene for about 30 seconds. A few moments later, he turned and came out, softly closing the door behind him. Then he turned to the other officer and said, "You go in and stop it." After the other officer took one brief look inside, he quickly shut the door. He didn't know what to do either! They both left the building muttering something to us about, "Whenever you can, try and quiet things down."

I was sure glad they were gone. If there is anything that could quench the Spirit of God in a Teen Challenge Chapel meeting filled with drug addicts, it would be the sight of a uniformed policeman standing at the door gawking inside!

It takes more power than the New York City police force or the opposition of a neighborhood to stop the work of the Holy Spirit—especially when He is at work rehabilitating the wrecked lives of the addicted and convicted.

Countless visitors from around the world have beaten a path to the door of our Teen Challenge Centers to see close up and firsthand the "unique cure" we offer to incurable drug addicts and alcoholics. The truth is that what happens in our centers is no more special than what happens anywhere else Christ is exalted, the Holy Spirit revealed, and the Father worshiped in "Spirit and in truth"! The only difference in our case is that nearly everyone in our "congregations" is in need of a radical spiritual revolution in their lives.

Our mode of "therapy" is considered unconventional and unprofessional by many. If and when we're asked to be "certified" by state drug agencies, every time they do not see so-called professional therapists, social workers, or psychologists on staff, they arbitrarily dismiss us as "unqualified" for certification. Their decision, in turn, makes us ineligible for government funding. It is ironic that God's "therapy" *works*—and is provided free of charge, while theirs usually doesn't work at all (although it comes with a very high price tag).

I received a call one day at the Brooklyn Center from a news reporter wanting to know "how many psychologists we had on the staff." My mother was working as the secretary, and she took the call. When she heard the question, she handed the phone to me. I quickly answered, "Oh, we have two psychologists on staff," and then I answered some additional questions for him as well.

When I hung up the phone, my mother directed a puzzled glance at me and asked who the two "psychologists" were—as if she hadn't already guessed. "Why, David and me, Mom! Don't you know we're Holy Ghost psychologists?" I said, with a twinkle in my eye. She just smiled and shook her head (she was a seasoned veteran).

Honestly, I have never doubted our qualifications to operate a program for drug addicts; nor will I ever apologize for our methods! Whenever we become too professional, too organized, or too dependent on methodology to trust in the Holy Spirit—even if the methodology has a "Christian" label—we will become just another ministry that began in the Spirit and ended up in the flesh!

We are not opposed to professional *Christian* counselors—some of our local centers use their skilled services. However, we don't want "the tail wagging the dog." We are determined to never turn our program over to those who *depend more on counseling techniques than on the power of God* through the work of the Holy Spirit!

Those rowdy Teen Challenge chapel meetings are the heart of the ministry! Worship is to a Christian rehabilitation program what group therapy is to a secular program—only it is more powerful. The "therapy of praise" is the way the residents deal with their inner feelings, longings, hurts, and wounds. They unburden their soul to the One who understands them better than anyone else ever did or could!

Praise and worship usher us into the presence of the Lord, and in His presence is "fulness of joy" (Ps. 16:11)! I have seen many "hard-case" residents who weren't moved in the least by my counseling or motivated by discipline or punishment who, nevertheless, were melted into submission in a worship service when the Holy Spirit moved in power! Again, we realize there is a genuine need for personal counseling at times—our programs do their share of it—but counseling can never substitute for the supernatural work of the Holy Spirit!

Whenever someone doubts the importance of the Holy Spirit's work, I just point to Victor, a tall Polish drug addict who was giving our staff fits. He could be the friendliest guy in the place one moment, but his volatile temper could explode in the next! When he put his fist through a door, I knew it was time for him to either leave or change.

When I called Victor into my office, he came in like a big puppy dog that knew he was in the doghouse. He flashed a big smile and said, "I guess I'm in trouble, right?" I didn't say anything because I was quietly praying for guidance from the Holy Spirit. I trusted Him to show me what to do. I've learned over the years that counseling and program manuals can't always tell you what to do at such times.

"Victor, where do you see yourself in the future?" I felt led to ask him. He pointed at me as I sat behind my desk, and I caught on immediately. "So you want my job?" I smiled. "Well, not right now! But someday I'd like to direct a Teen Challenge program," he said, looking just as serious as he could be. The thought flashed through my mind, *Victor, you're not even saved, and you want to be a director!* I immediately recognized the motivation behind such a seemingly foolish ambition—deep down inside, Victor wanted to help others.

Of course, first things had to come first. Victor first needed to find help himself and allow the Holy Spirit to change him. Armed with the hidden knowledge of Victor's inner motivations, I pulled my chair up and leaned toward him: "Victor, you can't go on like this. You either have to get saved or get out." I don't recommend this as the way to handle most situations of this kind, but I knew I was being directed by the Holy Spirit. When I told Victor to "get saved or get out," he simply looked at me and said, "Yes, sir." Then he asked to be excused.

I didn't see Victor until two days later, when he showed up in a church where I was conducting a service with a team from Teen Challenge to present our ministry to the congregation. Victor was there. When the pastor asked for testimonies, Victor was the first one to stand! He looked at me, and then at the congregation, and said, "You told me to get saved—and I did."

He had accepted Christ the night before at the center, but I did not know it until I walked in the church and heard his testimony—the first he'd ever given!

There are many other ways that the Holy Spirit works in the daily lives of our students. As they immerse themselves in prayer, worship, and praise, He faithfully meets them where they are to help them deal with the nitty gritty problems in their lives. This ministry is crucial. If these problems are not faced and overcome today, then they will overtake and overcome them in the difficult days to come—and they just might lead them right back to drugs.

John Macey, our Teen Challenge Director in Great Britain, wrote in his excellent book, *Tough Love*, about the Teen Challenge program and the 14 basic Bible studies used to disciple new converts.[1]

"Bernie, from the valley of South Wales, was as close to a madman as we were likely to meet. His search for life had taken him into every type of drug abuse, introduced him to the occult and alienated him from his family. After a session dealing with the principle of restitution, Bernie said, 'Pastor, I've got a guitar at home I stole from a club about four years ago and now I must give it back. I've decided I've got to do it, Pastor. I'm prepared to go back to the Blackwood Police

Station with the guitar, but I'd like you to come with me, if you will, please.'

"The Duty Sergeant at the police station recognized Bernie. 'What brings you here again?' he asked rather roughly. Bernie explained, and the sergeant looked at Bernie very strangely and left us. A few minutes later he reappeared blowing a layer of dust off the file he was carrying. 'This case was put away four years ago and would never have been reopened. What on earth's brought you here today to confess?' the policeman asked.

"Bernie said, 'Well, sir, it's like this. Since I last saw you I've become a born-again Christian and this business has been a barrier to my spiritual progress. I know I can't go any further with the Lord until I've dealt with it. I want to make a confession and then accept whatever punishment's necessary.'

"Bernie turned to me and grinned, 'I bet he thinks I'm mad. Last time he saw me in here I had filthy long hair, dirty clothes, and was drunk. Normally by now I'd have been thrown in the slammer for a few hours before they'd even see me. Things have changed a bit, eh?' he said proudly."[2]

Weeks later, an Inspector delivered an oral warning to Bernie, and according to Macey, "For the next 20 minutes we were able to witness to this local policeman about the work God was doing in so many of the men at the Center. We left the station convinced that God had used the situation to bring glory to His name, and returned to the Center to share the good news of the way in which the Lord had honored Bernie's faith. Such evidences of God's unfailing love were milestones too in our developing programme."[3]

The teaching of God's Word, coupled with the inward work of the Spirit, produces changes in our residents. Sometimes we saw gigantic transformations of character and conduct; sometimes they were just minuscule.

In Christian circles today, counseling techniques and psychology are often favored over allowing the Holy Spirit to move and work in those who have deep emotional and psychological wounds. But there is no substitute for dependency on the Holy Spirit. The truth is that there needs to be a good balance between preaching, teaching, counseling, and praise and worship. The latter, I believe, prepares the way for good counseling and preaching.

One of my professors in Bible college used to say, "All Word and you dry up, all Spirit, and you blow up. Word and Spirit and you grow up." When the Holy Spirit is the Teacher and Counselor, the effects are deep and supernatural in nature! Gary Almy and Carol Tharp Almy, in their book, *Addicted to Recovery*, wrote: "When the church holds the diamonds of Scripture in its hands, why does it go elsewhere for counsel?"[4]

Teaching classes are an essential part of every Teen Challenge program. David Batty began as a rehabilitation worker with me in Brooklyn during our pioneer days.

We were using standard Bible material typical of what was being used in churches and Sunday schools. But it was too "churchy" and it wasn't relevant—especially in terms of its illustrations and applications to the life and death problems faced by most drug addicts.

Under Dave Batty's direction, we developed Bible teaching material that was scriptural, yet culturally and academically geared to our target group. We approached the task in the same way missionaries adapt teaching to other "people groups" in foreign cultures. One graduate told me, "It was the classes and teaching that got me rooted in Christ. I think the majority of my class[mates] are still living for the Lord today because we had a teacher that poured the Word of God into us."

There are many Christian drug programs in place around the world today besides Teen Challenge. Those with the greatest potential for bearing "fruit that remains" are those that require their students to complete their classes, and those that don't send the residents out to do "fund raising" at the expense of being taught.

Whenever Christian rehabilitation "programs" are based more on secular therapeutic techniques rather than on the unchanging Word of God, that is the day the cross will no longer prevail over the switchblade and the narcotic needle! The "program" at Teen Challenge must never deteriorate into a system of "works," in which the staff or the students think that going to chapel, going to class, or getting good grades will make them righteous or holy. The prophet Zechariah declared, "[It is] not by might, nor by power, but by My spirit, saith the Lord of hosts" (Zech. 4:6b).

People who do not understand the spiritual components of our program often think the "program" itself somehow works the "cure." The fact is that the only "cure" is found in the person of Jesus Christ, the unchanging Word of God, and the supernatural work of the Holy Spirit. These secular observers often confuse the "therapy of praise" with other forms of therapy. At one Teen Challenge Center, a visitor thought she heard the students singing, "I've got brains. I've got brains." She was deeply impressed because she assumed she was witnessing a group therapy session based on a self-esteem chant! In fact, the residents were singing, "Our God reigns. Our God reigns!"

One of the dangers of an in-resident program like Teen Challenge, which incorporates both a structured daily program of spiritual as well as practical activity, is that the residents become *program dependent*. They may feel that the only way they can really be successful is by remaining in the program. We don't want them to make "the program" a form of escape, or to substitute their need for drugs with a new dependency on our "program." The only dependence we encourage is lifelong dependence on Jesus Christ, God the Father, and the Holy Ghost!

I spoke to one resident one day and asked, "How's it going?" He looked at me and said, "It's a struggle. I'm learning a lot about myself that's not good. But the Holy Spirit is working on me. He's putting the pressure on me." Then he asked me, "Tell me—how long does this go on? How long is the program?"

I looked closely at this six-foot-three-inch black brother, and smiled before I said, "Oh, the program! Well, it lasts the rest of your life."

He looked puzzled, so I said, "Let me explain. I am in *the program* just like you are! The 'program' is not Teen Challenge—the program is *Jesus*! So the 'program' goes with you wherever you go. You're in a lifelong program, and that is 'Jesus.' He is in you for the rest of your life."

Raul struggled with the whole idea of trying to "make it" outside the Teen Challenge safety zone (I helped him write a book about his story; it's entitled, *Raul*). To complicate matters, he still had the drug habit and craving *in his mind* even months after entering the program—and he knew it. He had accepted the Lord. He faithfully completed his class studies. He knew all the Scriptures about victory over sin. Yet, he knew he wasn't totally free.

No amount of counseling, teaching, or anything else he'd tried had given Raul the power to overcome what he called the "hammer." The "hammer" was the nagging, gnawing memory of what a shot of dope felt like. He just couldn't seem to shake it. Raul had come into the program and accepted the Lord, but left thinking he was ready for the outside world. He was not. He fell even deeper into drugs. Then he came back a second time. Raul writes that although he had a personal relationship with Jesus Christ, the addiction to drugs was still in his mind. He kept thinking about dope and fantasizing about 'getting off' shooting drugs, both at night and during the day. He continues:

> "Yet I couldn't shake the 'hammer.' Like some recovering alcoholics who never find freedom from the alcoholic personality and with one drink are right back to a state of alcoholism, I was physically clean and sober as far as absence of drugs in my body, but the drug craving—the mind habit— was still present with me."[5]

Raul was still in the rehabilitation program at the Teen Challenge Farm near Rehrersburg, Pennsylvania, when he finally won his freedom. Raul's freedom came in and through the "therapy of praise" while he was attending a black Pentecostal church in Harrisburg, Pennsylvania:

> "In the evening service we felt a mighty presence of the Lord from the outset...the pastor called our whole choir forward [Raul was participating in the service as part of a Teen Challenge choir from the Farm] and asked the members of the congregation to come and lay hands on us for prayer. As the pastor and elders prayed, and the believers laid hands on us asking the Lord to 'keep us' and make us 'strong,' I felt the power of God come upon me unlike I'd ever experienced. I'd been blessed before, but this was extra special.

"Even after returning back to the center late that night the afterglow of what happened lingered on. I didn't want to go to bed and put the blessing to sleep with me.

"I woke up with what I used to hear Don Wilkerson refer to as the new 'hang-over.' What God did the night before hung over the next day.

"When I knelt the next morning for my usual devotions and prayer something was different. The 'hammer' was gone! The mental desire for drugs and a high was no longer in my mind. 'Is this it?' I wondered. I prayed with a new freedom. Thirty minutes later it [the 'hammer'] was still gone. 'Praise God I'm totally free! The pressure isn't there anymore. Thank you, Lord. I'm free indeed!' "[6]

It was in this Holy Spirit atmosphere that Raul experienced true "deliverance." This was no "one-time emotional high"; it was a permanent miracle of grace! This kind of therapy is not based on the dependency of a group meeting or a therapist session. The therapy of praise is based on a divine encounter with the living God. One thing I feared as we began to develop the Christian approach to rehabilitation is that we would end up creating our own kind of Christian therapy based on the Teen Challenge "program."

In other words, I was afraid we would begin to believe we could "program" the residents toward change. We do have a daily schedule, a routine, and certain rules and regulations that must be followed. But following the "program" in and of itself does not produce change. Raul was religious in his adherence to the "program." He learned discipline, and he developed good work habits and a knowledge of God's Word through the daily classes. But the "hammer" was still in his head. It took a supernatural work of the Holy Spirit to remove that!

Now you know why the chapel services are the heart of Teen Challenge. Unless the Spirit is moving—the "program" will quickly deteriorate to mere "works" that are powerless to save anyone, especially those in heavy bondage!

We are not interested in creating a "hot house" Christianity in which our residents move from one kind of "high" to another spiritual "high." It doesn't help addicts to simply replace a drug high with a "Jesus high" that won't help them survive on the street. Our chapel services are not meant to be "pep rallies" that just charge up the emotions. Neither are they to be "lecture meetings" designed to "educate" a person toward rehabilitation. Only the Holy Ghost has the power to forever loose an addict from his "fix" and set his feet on an unmoving Rock. It is only because of the supernatural work of the Holy Spirit that Raul is still free today. He is not only free, but also the pastor of a thriving church ministering to the "Fourth World," and the director of a successful drug and alcohol rehabilitation program for men and women in Connecticut.

Endnotes

1. The National Teen Challenge office has specifically written Bible lessons for those with life-controlling problems. They are used by most local Teen Challenge Centers and are available for local churches to use as well. For information, write: National Teen Challenge, P.O. Box 1015, Springfield, MO 65801.

2. John Macey, *Tough Love* (Cumbria, United Kingdom: Send the Light, Ltd., 1992), pp. 68-70.

3. Macey, *Tough Love*, pp. 68-70.

4. Gary and Carol Tharp Almy, *Addicted to Recovery* (Eugene, Oregon: Harvest House Publishers, 1994), p. 22.

5. kaul Gonzalez, *Raul: A True Story*. (Shippensburg, Pennsylvania: Treasure House, 1989), pp. 133-134.

6. Gonzalez, *Raul*, p. 134.

Chapter 6

Free Indeed!

One of the most controversial questions and issues addressed in David's book, *The Cross and the Switchblade*, concerned the "baptism of the Holy Spirit." The controversy continues today, and critics and fans alike still want to know what part the "baptism" plays in helping someone break free from life-controlling problems such as drug or alcohol addiction, pornography, gambling, lying, cursing, smoking, or compulsive eating disorders.

When people examine the ministry of Teen Challenge, they often ask, "Does the baptism of the Holy Spirit play an important role in helping former drug addicts or alcoholics get off drugs? Will it really help them stay 'clean' once they kick their habit?"

I have personally observed thousands of lives in crisis over the past four decades, and I have come to some definite convictions on the matter. First, let me define the "baptism of the Holy Spirit" as a supernatural experience in which Christ fills a believers with a new power after they are born again in Christ. This gift is evidenced by the outward physical sign of speaking in other tongues according to Acts 2:4. The "baptism" also provides a new strength to boldly witness for Christ in word and in deed as He promised in Acts 1:8: "But ye shall receive power, after that the Holy Ghost is come upon you: and ye shall be witnesses unto Me...."

Early on in our work with drug addicts, we discovered the importance of the "Pentecostal Baptism" as a vital tool to help addicts fight the "battle of the mind" and break the emotional and mental grip of drugs, alcohol, and other temptations. It is still a vital tool today, but I am sad to say that in the ranks of Teen Challenge people and in Pentecostal churches at large, fewer and fewer believers lay claim to the Holy Ghost baptism. If this trend continues in our centers, I firmly believe the high success rate we have experienced in the past will rapidly diminish.

It is time once again to ask the question, "Does the baptism of the Holy Spirit help addicts overcome their problems, and does it help them have ongoing victory over drugs?" I'm willing to pose the question again and again *because I am absolutely sure about the answer*!

In the early days of this ministry, we repeatedly saw young men struggle and completely fail during the first few days of drug withdrawal—in spite of our fervent prayers, Scripture training, and passionate pleas for them to stay and see the process through. If you have ever worked with people like this, then you know how devastating it is to see someone come and go without finding freedom in Christ. It is one of the most difficult tests a Teen Challenge worker will ever face. You would almost do anything to keep these fragile victims from failing again.

It is hard not to get down and discouraged when you have worked for days or weeks (in some cases, even months) with someone and watched him open himself to the Lord for a period—only to see him suddenly and unexpectedly disappear. We have found that 90 percent of the addicts who give up prematurely are back in their old addictive lifestyles within hours of leaving the center. Others seemingly accept Christ and even manage to graduate from the program, yet they also fall back to their old life. We knew there had to be a better way.

As my brother struggled with this difficult question, someone suggested, "Why don't you talk to the boys who have come off of drugs successfully? Maybe you'll find the key." David did just that, and he started his "research project" at the very beginning—he talked with Nicky Cruz, the first Teen Challenge convert who had been deeply hooked on barbituates and marijuana before his conversion to Christ.

David told me, "I asked Nicky when it was that he felt he had victory over his old way of life. He told me something tremendous had happened to him at the time of his conversion on the street corner. He had been introduced at that time to the love of God. But it wasn't until later that he knew he had complete victory." When David asked, "And when was that, Nicky?"

the former gang leader said, "At the time of my baptism in the Holy Spirit."

This discovery at the early stages of our work with addicts has proven true over four decades of work around the world in every culture and language group. The baptism of the Holy Spirit seems to be God's "designated" tool to help those in bondage of any kind to be "free indeed" following their conversion.

I have seen this proven countless times in the past 40 years or so. Pastor Jack Hayford described the *purpose* of the baptism in the Holy Spirit in his excellent book, *The Beauty of Spiritual Language*:

1. It is an intended resource when I know a difficult situation is coming up.
2. It is a refreshing in the midst of spiritual warfare.
3. It is a means of imbibing strength when facing temptation, or as a means of inviting God's wisdom when needing to make a decision. [1]

Pastor Hayford's analysis is borne out in an incident involving a Teen Challenge resident named Tony. His first spiritual warfare encounter was dramatic and humorous.

Tony had come back to the Brooklyn Teen Challenge Center from our rehabilitation farm in Pennsylvania for a weekend pass. He was about "four months old" in the Lord and in the Teen Challenge resident program. We felt he deserved a chance to go home on his own to visit his family, even though they lived in "El

Barrio," or Spanish Harlem, a place that was notorious for widespread drug addiction and prostitution.

Before Tony left the Brooklyn Center for a four-hour "pass," he came and spoke to me. "Brother Don, I'm scared! I know I'm probably going to meet up with some of my old addict friends, and I just don't know if I'm strong enough. What do I do?"

I said, "Tony, you've already done all that's necessary. You're saved, correct?" (I didn't even need an answer; I knew he was.) "And you're filled with the Holy Spirit! Now go ahead and head for home, because 'Greater is He that is in you, than he that is in the world'!" (1 Jn. 4:4b)

Tony quietly slipped into the chapel and spent a few moments in prayer before he headed down the street to the subway for the ride to upper Manhattan. Later that day, he returned within the allowed time and came through the door with a smile from ear to ear!

"God did a miracle for me," he almost shouted. "What happened to you?" I asked. "Well, when I got off the subway and started walking down my block—I saw no one! No one was on the streets. I mean, none of my old drug addict friends or acquaintances were in sight. I couldn't believe it: No pushers! No prostitutes! Everyone else was out on the streets, but none of *them*. I made it all the way in my apartment without seeing anyone, and when I sat on the living room couch, I breathed a sign of relief and told the Lord, 'Thank You for clearing the streets for me.'"

I smiled and thanked the Lord for helping Tony deal with temptation—by supernaturally removing it! But Tony's story didn't end there!

"But that was not it, Brother Don!" Tony said, interrupting me in his excitement. "That is not how God helped me deal with temptation. Just listen to what happened on my way home! My parents were glad to see me. I ate some rice and beans. Then it was time to come back. I went outside and stood on the stoop. I looked down one side of the street, then the other, and again, I saw no one."

The intensity and joy in Tony's eyes grew brighter as he continued: "Then I carefully started walking to the subway. I was almost ready to go down the stairs, and wham! I don't know where he came from, but there was Sonny, one of the old timers! He was a real dope fiend and the biggest pusher in the neighborhood."

"He said to me, 'Wow, Tony, you look good! Glad to see you back.' I knew what he was thinking, Brother Don," Tony told me. "He saw me all clean-looking, and he noticed that I'd gained weight. He figured I must have just got out of the hospital or jail. Then he offered to sell me a bag of heroin," Tony explained, his face now intense as he relived the scene he'd experienced only 45 minutes earlier.

"Sonny asked me, 'You want to buy a bag of stuff?' Then he pulled it out quickly for me to see, and then pushed it right back in his pocket. When I saw the dope, I froze," Tony told me. "I thought, *This is it! This is the moment I have dreaded.* This was the temptation I had feared I would face if I went back into my old neighborhood."

I waited anxiously for the rest of Tony's story. I knew he was not high, not at least under the influence of *drugs*...

Tony started laughing, and then he continued with a twinkle in his eye, "When Sonny asked me, 'You want to buy a bag of stuff?' I told him, 'No thank you—*I got my own stuff!*' Sonny got a surprised look on his face and said, 'Oh yeah? Where do you get your stuff now?' "

Tony looked at me with a grin and continued his story: "I told him, 'I get mine in Brooklyn.' Sonny really got interested, and he said, 'Brooklyn? I get to Brooklyn now and then. What's the address?' I told him, 'It's 416 Clinton Avenue,' " Tony said, laughing again. "I gave him the address of Teen Challenge!"

"Then he asked, 'Who's your connection?' " Tony added. "I told him right out—it's Jesus Christ," Tony said, as proud and firm as could be. "Sonny looked at me strangely for a moment. Then he said, 'Man, you're crazy,' then walked away. As he walked away, I said to him, 'No, you're crazy! *I don't need what you have anymore!*' "

Excited about his victory on the street, Tony said, "Brother Don, the Lord let it all happen just like that to show me His reality out there where it really counts! Now I really know that: "If the Son therefore shall make you free, ye shall be free indeed" (Jn. 8:36).

Tony's case may sound dramatic in some respects, but it is also typical. When he was faced with temptation, he had what I call a "Holy Ghost reaction." Tony didn't panic. When his old drug pusher asked, "Do you want to buy a bag of stuff?" Tony spoke out of his innermost being. The Jesus on the inside was working on the outside! The Holy Spirit had given Tony supernatural "No!" power—the power to resist temptation by saying "No!" to sin. The Holy Spirit didn't stop there—He also gave Tony "Yes!" power—the power to boldly proclaim, *"No thank you. I've got my own stuff!"*

You don't have to be a drug addict on the streets of El Barrio to understand this. The devil has "stuff" for everyone. Tony's "stuff" happened to be "heroin." Every Christian has to deal with the devil's "stuff," and one person's temptation may not be another's. The devil knows better to tempt me with drugs or alcohol, but he knows my weak points! He has had his pushers trying to push the "stuff" that fuels my personal weaknesses onto me, and he's tried to push "stuff" on you as well.

Those who have confessed Christ as their Savior have both an inward cleansing and a power to deal with whatever satan throws at them. Christ provided our forgiveness through the cross and by His resurrection. Scripture says, "And if the Spirit of Him who raised Jesus from the dead is living in you, He who raised Christ from the dead will also give life to your mortal bodies through His Spirit, who lives in you" (Rom. 8:11 NIV).

Jesus also gave us the baptism of the Holy Spirit to help us have power over sin and its ongoing temptation.

Tony went out into the battlefield of temptation armed with both the "shield of faith" and the baptism of the Holy Ghost described in Acts 1:8 and 2:4.

My brother, David, explains it this way:

"From the beginning of Christianity, then, this baptism of the Holy Ghost has had a special significance because it marks the difference between the mission of a mere man, no matter how bold and effective, and the ministers of Christ: Jesus would baptize His followers with the Holy Ghost. In His last hours on earth, Jesus spent a great deal of time talking to His disciples about the Holy Ghost who would come after His death to stand by them, comfort them, lead them and give them that power which would allow them to carry His mission forward."[2]

David and I, along with countless numbers of Teen Challenge workers, have literally experienced this supernatural power in ourselves as we have labored over the years to rehabilitate people who were convinced that they were destined to live a life of addiction and alcoholism. The Holy Spirit gave us the strength and anointing to proclaim the gospel of Christ with power and authority.

This message is "Good News" for everyone who has "fallen short of the glory of God." It is especially important for individuals whose sins have so bound them in addictive habits and compulsive behavior that they think they cannot function apart from that activity.

Once the "Good News" of salvation in Jesus Christ has been received, we have learned to immediately introduce new converts to the Holy Spirit baptism. It seems to equip and arm these victims of bondage with a supernatural "weapon of God"! This supernatural weapon helps them overcome the inevitable temptations brought along by the evil forces trying to pull them back into their "old way of life."

When a Catholic priest visited our center to learn about the baptism of the Holy Spirit for the first time, one resident told him, "With me, He [Jesus] helped me get rid of drugs. I used to use goof balls and marijuana, and I was beginning to skin pop heroin [by injecting heroin under the skin of the upper arm with a hypodermic needle]. I already had the mind habit, and I just had to do this thing. When I heard about Jesus, it kind of shocked me that He loved people in spite of all their sins. It stirred me when I heard that He puts teeth behind His promises by coming into us with the Holy Spirit. They told me the Holy Spirit is called the Comforter. Now when I thought of comfort, I used to think of a bottle of wine and half-a-dozen barbituates. But these guys were talking about comfort out of Heaven, where I could feel clean later."

I explain to Teen Challenge residents the importance of "walking in the Spirit" and "being filled with the Spirit" this way: When an addict falls, he or she falls *hard*—real hard. Other backsliders may go back to smoking cigarettes, living a promiscuous life, or serving the idols of this world. These are certainly destructive in and of themselves. An addict, on the other hand, goes back to a lifestyle that is potentially deadly. I'm not just talking about moral and spiritual health—the addict's lifestyle threatens his very emotional and physical well-being.

When an addict goes back on drugs, he faces possible death through an overdose, by contracting AIDS, or by spending years in a jail someplace. This is why converted addicts have even more reasons than normal converts to maintain a fervent, vibrant, and up-to-date daily walk with the Lord—*they have a lot more to lose* if they fall back into sin.

Teen Challenge residents go through hours of daily Bible classes and daily chapel services. We also give them time in their daily schedule for personal devotions. The three square meals they receive to restore health to their physical bodies after coming off drugs must be equally balanced with three good spiritual meals daily! In a way, they are on a spiritual "crash course" or combat boot camp, designed to prepare them for their ongoing war against satan.

The statistics of over 40 years of ministry dramatically prove this point: Those who open themselves totally to Jesus as their Savior *and* Lord, and who seek the baptism of the Holy Spirit, have the *best hope of leaving their drug past behind them* when they leave the program after a year or so.

One day I received an unusual visitor at the Brooklyn Center. A social worker doing field research on drug addiction asked me if she could conduct some private interviews with one of our residents. I knew she was skeptical, so I picked a particular young man with enough street smarts to catch her skepticism and witness in a creative way.

He did just that. After this social worker had asked this young man many questions about his old drug patterns and lifestyle of a drug addict, she asked him, "What is different about this place?" He had already told her that he had been in other secular programs, but hadn't found the help he needed in those programs.

"What do they do for you here, or what do they give you here in the way of therapy, that you didn't get in other programs?" she asked. "Well, let me put it this way," he said. "They give us God in the morning, Jesus in the afternoon, and the Holy Ghost at night."

The young woman didn't know how to respond at first, then she asked, "But do you think you're using God as a crutch?" He was quick to respond. "You can call it whatever you want. If it is a crutch, give me two of them!" (In reality, there are three of them: God the Father; His Son, Jesus; and the Holy Spirit!)

Endnotes

1. Jack Hayford, *The Beauty of Spiritual Language* (Dallas, Texas: Word, 1992), p. 137.

2. Wilkerson, *The Cross and the Switchblade*, pp. 156-157.

Chapter 7

The "Icing on the Cake"

The baptism of the Holy Spirit serves two vital purposes in the lives of believers: the inward work of holiness, and the provision of an explosive power to "be" a witness of God's grace to the world. Victor Torres was a converted drug addict who recognized the call of God upon his life, yet he felt an urgent need for *more power* to fulfill that call. He longed to reach out to others who were still trapped in the bondage of addiction, but he simply felt too timid and powerless to answer the call.

Victor's very personality changed once he was baptized in the Holy Spirit! The once bashful ex-Roman Lord gang member and drug addict suddenly was transformed into a bold proclaimer of the gospel after he was filled with the Spirit! When Victor first came to the Brooklyn Teen Challenge Center, the tall and skinny addict received an immediate freedom from drugs and other bad habits. But when it came to fulfilling this call, he needed more.

Victor told me, "I gained a lot of respect for Nicky Cruz as he helped me in the growing process. He became my model. I recognized him to be a man of God. Nobody in the center could put anything over on him. In chapel he told us, 'God's angels have a telescope and they're looking at you all the time, checking you out. Don't be phony, and don't try to fool God. You'll end up being the fool!' He understood us, and his message got through."[1]

Victor's life was about to change even more. He told me, "After two weeks at the center, Nicky said, 'Victor, do you want to get out of the city and go to our special training program in Pennsylvania?' After careful instruction, I felt ready to go." Nicky and Victor left the city, and three hours later they drove up "God's Mountain" (the small hill on which that training center is located).

"I joined guys from the same lifestyle I'd led," Victor said. "They, like I, had accepted the Lord. After being assigned a room and meeting my new roommates, I took a walk to explore the woods, the fields, and the barn. I collected my thoughts as I strolled. Things had changed drastically and dramatically in two weeks. Before then, I used to sniff dope into my nostrils; now I was filling my lungs with pure air. As I made my way to the highest point on the hill and looked out over the greenery, I compared it all with Brownsville, Brooklyn, and Powell Street [the ghetto he lived in for 15 years]— and I cried for joy!"

"Sometimes I remained in the chapel for several hours, seeking the Lord and asking Him to fill me with the Spirit of power and love in a new way," Victor said.

"On other occasions, seven or eight of the guys would gather in someone's room to pray late into the night. At one of those prayer times, my friend Mingo received the prayer language of the Spirit. I was both happy and upset about it at the same time. I asked the Lord, 'Why is it that Mingo got saved after me, but You baptized him before me? Didn't I deserve it first?' Now I was more anxious than ever to receive."

A few weeks later, a visiting minister spoke on the same subject in chapel. Victor told me, "As he preached about 'the Pentecostal power, the old-time power, and the fire of Pentecost,' I got excited! By the time he came to the end of a song about this 'power,' I felt raised six inches off the pew—and closer to the Lord," Victor recalled. "The preacher came down off the platform, pointed at me, and said, 'Young man, you're going to receive the baptism of the Holy Spirit!' That was all I needed to release my faith. The stopper was pulled and the river of living water flowed out of my innermost being! Something came over me. I felt as if I had left the world for a few moments. I knew where I was (I was fully conscious)—and yet I knew I was in touch with another world. Then I spoke in other tongues!"

"While I was praising Him in this new language, God gave me a vision," Victor said. "Whether it was in my mind or with my eyes, I do not know, nor does it matter. The effect and reality of it were the same. A big cloud came down on a corn field, and an individual was in the middle of the cloud. I could not see the face, but people were worshiping the One in the middle. Then I saw the cloud go up to Heaven and disappear. I knew I had experienced the nearness of the Lord Jesus like I never had before. Then I thought, *If this is the joy we get down here on earth when the Spirit makes Jesus real, how much greater will it be in Heaven?*"

"The infilling of the Holy Spirit affected me in various ways," Victor explained. "It broke down my fear of speaking out for Christ. It loosed me from a psychological bondage. I wasn't afraid anymore to testify personally to individuals about what the Lord had done for me, and what He could do for them."

"When Brother Reynolds [the executive director at the time] invited me to give my testimony at a high school assembly, not even the 1,500 faces staring at me could hold me back!" Victor exclaimed. "There was a burning fire in me. The words flowed as though they were coming from a living fountain within! I made the mistake of not shutting off the fountain in time, and I began telling the students about the baptism of the Holy Spirit and speaking in other tongues. Brother Reynolds finally pulled my coattail. I felt embarrassed, yet at the same time, I was happy to tell the whole world, 'Jesus is alive!' "

Victor told me he received a call from his parents soon after that, and he told them about his experience with the baptism of the Holy Spirit. "I didn't exalt this experience above salvation, but for a former drug addict like me who had lived on 'highs' most of his life, the baptism in the Spirit showed me that I could experience Christ in a dramatic, euphoric, and yet glorious fashion—as well as learning the life of dedication, discipline, and truth!"

Victor added, "Since then, I have learned that the most important part of being a Christian is in the walk—the life of obedience, of following the teaching of Christ. Yet there are spiritual 'highs' as I refer to them, along our journey (if we want them)." Then Victor told me, "Some Christians feel they don't need the Spirit's infilling, or that it is not the will of God for them, and I respect their opinion. But I thank God, first for my salvation and deliverance from sin, which, of course, included taking drugs. Then I am also thankful that the Spirit saw my inner needs and gave me a manifestation of His power. *It was the icing on the cake!*"[2]

If the Holy Spirit baptism is the "icing on the cake," as Victor Torres described it, then the "cake" is Jesus. Victor's personal testimony makes that clear. Jesus is not and should never be used as the "dessert" of life—*He is the main course.* True salvation through Christ involves a change within that results in the fruits of love, joy, peace, and other practical outward manifestations. The best way to help these young converts who have been baptized in the Holy Spirit to produce the genuine fruit of the Spirit in their lives is to bring personal discipline and maturity into their new walk in Christ.

I often tell residents in the midst of their discipleship training, "I don't care how loud you shout in the chapel! If you really know Jesus, then you *must* speak the truth in love outside the chapel with your brothers and sisters! I don't care how high you jump inside the chapel (if you do jump)—*make sure you walk straight when you land!*"

One of the ways we know a resident is *really* converted and changed is by his *attitude toward work*. Many drug addicts and substance abusers will readily admit that they only worked "angles" in their past life. "Working" for them meant scheming, conniving, and doing whatever they could get away with to get money for drugs. In their new life in Christ, all of them must learn to be disciplined in their work habits. The Teen Challenge residential program is geared to test every resident in this area.

In addition to such daily chores as mopping floors, cleaning windows, doing dishes, peeling potatoes—and a lot of other things many have never done before—some long-term centers have established vocational projects or shops geared to teach productive work habits. In some cases, these vocational programs actually generate income for the ministry as a by-product of the training.

At one center, students wash and clean cars at an auto auction. At another, they grow strawberries and other cash crops. At the farm in Pennsylvania, there is a print shop, an auto mechanics shop, a small engine repair shop, and a T-shirt production facility, plus many other "shops." Our women's home in Budapest, Hungary, grows and sells mushrooms, and raises chickens for the work therapy and income it provides.

In Paraguay, Teen Challenge students make cinder blocks and publish a drug prevention magazine that they sell on the streets. Both projects generate income for this vital "Third World" based program. Within a year of this center's founding, it was almost completely self-supporting as far as its operational budget. Building funds and support for facility expansion must still come from outside sources.

We view the men and women in our centers as people created in God's image with untapped spiritual and human potential. It is our task to help them tap into this potential for the glory of God—both in the "here and now" and for eternity. Everything we do in Teen Challenge is geared toward the twofold goal of preparing our students and residents for Heaven *and* for earth! We are determined to prepare them to die right for eternity, and to live right in the here and now!

Endnotes

1. Today, Victor Torres is the pastor of New Life Outreach International church in Richmond, Virginia. He is also the founder and Executive Director of New Life for Youth, which includes a rehabilitation program for men and women that presently serves nearly a hundred residents.

2. Parts of this testimony are excerpted from *Son of Evil Street*, by Victor Torres with Don Wilkerson, 1995.

Chapter 8

The Grace of God
on Two Sides of the Door!

The names of Jim and Onesimus are forever linked together in my mind—one man is from the twentieth century, and the other is from the first century. They are linked together because both men experienced "the grace of God on the *other side of the door*."

Jim is a former cocaine user who grew up in a middle-class home. His father was a deacon in an Assembly of God church. Jim married and raised three lovely children, and his wife was very active in the church. Jim became a successful stock broker, but his business took him into the world of high finance—and designer drugs. At the end of a busy day of trading, most of the brokers headed for the local bar. The drinkers hung out in the front, and the cocaine sniffers stayed in the back.

At first, Jim hung out in the front of the bar. Although he went to church, he had never made a full commitment of his life to Christ. Most of his acquaintances thought he was a Christian because he appeared to live such a moral life, though he drank.

When the economy took a downturn, it affected his job situation severely. Jim responded to the increased pressure on the job by hanging out in the back of the bar where, for the first time in his life, he did something he never believed he would do—he began to use cocaine.

"I think I was hooked immediately," he told me. "I was soon using all of my normal spending money on drugs. Eventually I dipped into a small savings account and drained that. I even borrowed against a pension plan, and in less than a month, spent it all on cocaine." Jim's wife was very naive at first, thinking her husband's change in behavior was due to the pressures of the job.

On the day she discovered that the money in their savings account was gone, Jim's wife woke up fast—and threw her husband out of the house. So he moved in with some so-called friends. "They were just a bunch of white-collar junkies themselves," Jim said. "Some were successful enough to support their habits while remaining on the job. I wasn't. When I lost my job, it devastated me. I suddenly realized I was a workaholic—my whole identity was tied to my job. When I lost that, along with losing my wife and children, I felt like I had nothing to live for anymore."

Jim began taking odd jobs—and drinking. "Since I couldn't really afford to use cocaine anymore, I 'graduated' downward," he said. "For two years, I lived life on the edge—the edge of homelessness, poverty, and suicide. I don't think I had enough courage even to commit suicide, or so I thought at the time. Now I realize it was the prayers of my family that kept me from totally destroying myself."

Jim came to realize that his addiction to alcohol was like "committing suicide on the installment plan." Little by little, he was sinking deeper and further into the muck and mire of an addictive lifestyle. Occasionally he had money for cocaine, but most of the time he drank.

"One night I was sitting in a bar looking through a local newspaper, and I saw an advertisement for the showing of *The Cross and the Switchblade* movie at a local church. I'd read the book as a teenager, and I even heard David Wilkerson speak at a crusade once. I decided to go to the movie." Then Jim related how events led up to a new beginning for him.

"I went to the church where they were showing the movie, and as the film began I realized I had seen it years before in a theater in our hometown when it first came out. But as I watched it this time, it was different. It was no longer the story of kids in trouble in the inner city. *It was my story.* I saw *myself* in certain places of the film." As Jim shared this with me, his eyes began to sparkle.

"When the movie finished, in fact, I couldn't wait for it to end because, somehow, I knew they were going to give an altar call. They did, and I went forward! For the first time in my life, I opened my heart to God and begged Him to save me and change me," he recalled. "You know, it's funny. When I was in the church before, it all seemed so boring. I was not interested. I went along with everything, but I guess I was just indifferent. I don't recall being rebellious, but now I realize

I was worse than being rebellious; I just didn't care, or sense my need for the Lord. But I did after watching *The Cross and the Switchblade*."

That night, Jim shared his situation with one of the staff ministers at the church, and he urged Jim to go into Teen Challenge. The next day he was there.

"It was hard, and humbling," Jim said. "Many of the guys came right off the street, and they came from a totally different background than me. At first I sort of kept myself aloof from them—after all, I'd been a stock broker, not a street junkie," Jim confessed. "But then the Holy Spirit rebuked me and showed me I was about to become the 'Pharisee' in the parable where Jesus compared the prayers of a Pharisee and a publican. The Pharisee prayed, 'God, I thank Thee, that I am not as other men are, extortioners, unjust, adulterers, or even as this publican' " (Lk. 18:11b).

"After that, I got in and among the other guys and tried to fit in, help them, and learn from them," Jim said. "I'd never been in a multiracial or multicultural environment before in my life. It was educational, as well as inspirational and instructional." It was while Jim was in the program that he began to pray that he and his wife be reconciled.

"I'd had no contact with her for two years, although I remembered my kids' birthdays and our anniversary. I called a few times, and if my wife answered the phone, I'd hang up; but if my children answered, I'd talk to them," Jim said, continuing his story. About six months after Jim's conversion, he and a few other men who had also lost their spouses because of their drug life were in a prayer meeting one night. "As I was praying, I felt a strong urge to go home and see my wife and children," Jim said.

Jim shared this with one of the Teen Challenge counselors the next day. "I didn't know how it would be received," he said, "but I thank God for that staff counselor. He told me, 'Well, Jim, I know you've been praying about this, and you know we've taught you that it's possible for you to hear the voice of the Lord. So if this is something you feel is from the Lord, then you better do it.'"

The visit was planned for the next weekend, and when the final day arrived, Jim took a bus to his hometown. All during the ride, he felt an excitement growing inside as he anticipated seeing his family again. "But as soon as I got off the bus," Jim said, "the enemy put a big-time fear in my mind! I guess it was fear of rejection, fear of the future, and fear of meeting my wife's family."

When Jim reached his hometown, he began walking aimlessly around the downtown area. "I walked and walked. I just could not bring myself to go down the street toward my house," he said. But Jim knew it would be worse to get back on the bus and go back to Teen Challenge without following through on his leading from the Lord.

"I had to find out," he shared. "I knew other guys who had tried to be reconciled—they had the door slammed in their face, their letters were never answered, and their phone calls were rejected. All of that was going through my mind.

"Then I remembered the prayer meeting, and I remembered how the prompting came to go home in the first place," Jim said. "Part of a verse from the Bible came to mind: 'In returning and rest shall ye be saved; in quietness and in confidence shall be your strength' " (Is. 30:15).

Finally Jim made his way to Wexford Avenue. "My knees were shaking as I walked up the path and climbed the steps to my house. The whole street was quiet and peaceful. I felt like I was living out a scene in a movie," he said.

When Jim finally knocked on the door of his home, the grace of God in his life was evident "on his side of the door." Would there be grace, forgiveness, and acceptance on the other side?

Jim's situation parallels another man's problem described in the pages of Bible history. Onesimus was a runaway slave who lived during the first century. His flight ultimately landed him in the city of Rome. Like most runaways, he probably hung out in the part of town where others like himself were hiding from the law. We don't know all the circumstances, but somehow Onesimus came in contact with the "rehab program" of his day, and the director was none other than the apostle Paul.

Paul was under house arrest in Rome at the time, awaiting trial before Caesar on charges of treason leveled by jealous Jewish leaders in Jerusalem. Since Paul was allowed to have house guests, he turned his "prison cell" into an evangelism-discipleship center. Paul's prison house also became a first century model for Teen Challenge-style outreach. Among the many visitors who visited him there was a runaway slave named Onesimus.

Young Onesimus, the fugitive on the run from his master and the law, the social castaway and personal failure, turned his life over to the control of Jesus Christ. It was at that point that Paul began the dramatic rehabilitation of Onesimus. The two became very, very close. In fact, they developed such a kinship (those of us who work in Teen Challenge understand this closeness between teacher and student, discipler and disciple, and counselor and counseled), that when it was time for Onesimus to "graduate," Paul found it very difficult to part with his "son in the faith."

The story of Onesimus is recorded in the apostle Paul's epistle entitled "Philemon." Of all Paul's letters, this is the most personal in nature. If you like opening and reading other people's mail, then you will love the Epistle to Philemon.

There are three relationships shared in this letter. The first is the close relationship between Paul and Onesimus. This was a full relationship that included two-way giving and receiving between Paul and Onesimus. Paul wrote that Onesimus "...ministered unto me in the bonds of the gospel" (Philem. 13). Onesimus was an educated man with the valuable ability to read and write clearly. One of the ways he served Paul was by writing out epistles and documents for him. In fact, Onesimus wrote this very letter addressed to his slave master!

The second relationship was between Paul and Philemon, the recipient of the letter. Philemon was a property and slave owner whom Paul had led to the Lord on one of his missionary journeys. A church even met in Philemon's home!

If you view these two relationships as parts of a triangle, then place Paul at the top of the triangle, put Philemon at the bottom right-hand corner, and Onesimus in the bottom left-hand corner. There is a line drawn between Paul and Onesimus, and a second line runs from Paul to Philemon. Something is missing. There is no line at the bottom of the triangle because the relationship between Philemon and Onesimus had been severed.

That relationship was broken and severed for the same reason the relationship between Jim and his wife, Karen, was broken. Jim had blown it. His addiction had separated and torn him away from his most important and intimate relationships.

Onesimus was the legal slave of Philemon. It is doubtful that Philemon kept an educated servant like Onesimus under chains or in locked quarters. He probably trusted his slave to honor his position in return for freedom of movement and certain rights in the household. Onesimus decided to face possible death under Roman law to run away from his legal master, thus breaking their relationship of trust. Since Paul offered to pay back anything Onesimus owed, it is probable that he had stolen money and goods as well (see Philem. 18-19).

As Paul discipled Onesimus, he realized that, just as in Jim's case, it was time for Onesimus to go home, "face the music," and repair the damage.

Judging by Paul's letter to Philemon, sending his "son in the faith," Onesimus, back to his master was probably one of the hardest things Paul had ever done. The risks were tremendous, for in those days, slavery was deeply ingrained in that society. There was an estimated 60 million slaves in the Roman Empire alone, and escaped slaves could be legally put to death or tortured at the whim of their masters. No one knew better than Paul what risks he was taking in sending Onesimus back to the very scene of his crimes.

A slave was not considered a person—he was a living "tool," somewhat like a piece of farm machinery. A master had absolute power over his slaves. They were deliberately held in check, since there was always the danger of revolt. It was for this reason that rebellious slaves were almost always promptly eliminated. If a slave ran away like Onesimus did, and if he was caught, at best he would be branded with a red-hot iron on the forehead with the letter "F" to mark him as a *fugitive* and *runaway*. At the worst, he would be crucified to death.

Paul knew all this. Slavery was such a part of the ancient world that even if a Christian slave willingly returned to a Christian master after running away, there was still no guarantee that he would be safe. It is amazing that Paul sent him, and that Onesimus went. Only the Holy Spirit could accomplish this miracle.

Picture Onesimus when the time came to knock at his master's door. Would Onesimus find grace on the other side of the door, or a lifetime of sorrow and servitude? I can almost see Onesimus' knees shaking. He wasn't just risking rejection; he could face painful death by law.

Onesimus went to the back door (after all, he was a slave). After he knocked at the door, a servant answered and quickly told his master. When Philemon came to the door, Onesimus immediately handed him Paul's letter and waited to learn his fate. Philemon accepted the scroll, broke the wax seal, and began to read these words in a handwritten script he recognized as the flowing style of Onesimus:

> *I beseech thee for my son Onesimus, whom I have begotten in my bonds: which in time past was to thee unprofitable, but now profitable to thee and to me: whom I have sent again: thou therefore receive him...*
(Philemon 10-12).

When Philemon reached the end of the letter, I think he looked up at Onesimus, and then back at the letter again. *Yes, Paul's signature is on it,* he must have thought.

We are not told if Philemon struggled over Paul's letter and Onesimus' conversion. We are left to use our imagination, but the spirit of Paul's letter, and his glowing description of Philemon as a man of God who demonstrated love and faith toward the Lord Jesus, and toward all the saints—gives us every reason to believe that Philemon opened his heart and door to his prodigal runaway (see Philem. 1-7,21).

Onesimus experienced the grace of God on *both sides* of the door. The outsider was given an insider's welcome. As Paul stated in verse 11, the "unprofitable" servant was now made "profitable." Onesimus' name literally means "profitable," but his life had turned unprofitable to Philemon until he was introduced to Jesus Christ by Paul. Now Onesimus ("Profitable") could live up to his name! In fact, Bible historians believe Onesimus was extended such grace and forgiveness by Philemon that he granted the runaway slave his freedom!

The triangle of relationship had been completed. Philemon, the born-again slave owner, became Onesimus' "brother" as Paul requested. Onesimus was no longer treated as a "slave" but as a "beloved brother." What about Jim? Did his story have the same positive ending as that of Onesimus? Here is the rest of his incredible testimony to God's grace!

The moment Jim knocked on the door of the home where he had enjoyed almost ten years of apparent success as a husband and father, and more recently a few heartrending years of utter failure, he had no letter from an apostle to hand to his wife. He stood on sheer faith—with a supernatural measure of divine grace.

Karen answered the door, and Jim sheepishly said, "Hi." His wife looked at him, and said nothing. "I felt awkward, and I almost ran away, the tension was so great," he said.

Then Karen quietly and softly said, "Come in." They stood and stared at each other for what seemed to be an endless period of time to Jim. When Karen finally went over to the couch, Jim took a seat across from her. "I'm glad you came, Jim," Karen said, breaking the awkward silence. Jim smiled and nodded his head, still not knowing what to say.

"I've...I've been in a place getting help, Karen. You may not believe this, but I've changed. Jesus changed me. I think—I mean—I am...a new man," Jim said, as he began to share his testimony. Then Karen interrupted him!

"We heard."

"You did?" Jim asked, sitting back in the chair. Then Karen explained that she had learned that Jim was in Teen Challenge through her pastor. Wisely, she had waited before getting her hopes up. Yet God had preserved her from bitterness. She did her best not to lie or cover up Jim's drug use and alcohol abuse with her children; but neither did she speak ill of him in their presence.

One of the ways she preserved the children from anger toward Jim for abandoning them was by joining them to pray for him regularly. When the kids expressed hope that Daddy would return some day, she never discouraged it. In fact, their childlike prayers of faith kept her own faith alive.

After about the fifth month of Jim's stay in Teen Challenge, Karen went to see one of the counselors in the church where Jim was saved. She wanted to find out if he was "for real" or not. The counselor called the center and was given a good report on Jim, which was shared with Karen.

"What should I do when he comes home...if he does come home?" she asked. "Oh, your heart will tell you what to do. You just keep praying for Jim. The Lord will show you what to do, and how to get your lives back together again," the counselor told her.

When the day finally came, Karen knew exactly what to do! She looked across the room at her prodigal husband and said, "Welcome home, Jim!"

"The children will sure be surprised when they get off the school bus. Why don't you go out to meet them?" Jim's wife suggested. "We all have a lot of catching up to do!" she said, with a big smile on her face.

Jim couldn't have asked for a better reception if he'd written the script himself, but he didn't! God personally wrote it for him, and now Karen and the three children were about to gain a lost husband and father!

Jim, like Onesimus, experienced the grace of God on *both sides of the door*. The outcast became the accepted; now an unprofitable father and husband had been given the opportunity to become "profitable."

These two stories from different centuries and different circumstances point out that one of the most important and remarkable by-products of a newborn soul and life is the miraculous restoration of broken relationships. I can't repeat this enough: the gospel in the heart not only prepares us for Heaven, but also for earth! It prepares us to not only die right, but to love right!

The Teen Challenge ministry constantly sees husbands returned to their wives, fathers returned to their children, and children restored to their parents. This is a direct fulfillment of the prophecy in the Book of Malachi (the last verses in the Old Testament):

See, I will send you the prophet Elijah before that great and dreadful day of the Lord comes. He will turn the hearts of the fathers to their children, and the hearts of the children to their fathers; or else I will come and strike the land with a curse (Malachi 4:5-6 NIV).

Our nations are now laboring under the pain and burden of growing numbers of fatherless children and families who have been abandoned—but Christ can restore these fallen men to their rightful place in their marriages and homes. I have probably conducted marriages for as many divorced couples as any minister I know. That is, I have remarried couples to their "original spouses" after they had been divorced as a result of drug addiction breaking up the home and marriage.

One of the first questions I am often asked when a Teen Challenge resident gives his life to Jesus Christ is: "Do you think God can bring my family back together?" I have seen this happen too many times to ever doubt God.

Not every Teen Challenge story has a happy ending like Jim's or Onesimus' in the Bible. In some cases, due to the remarriage of a spouse, or the spouse's unwillingness to forgive and start over again, it is impossible, in the natural, to see some marriages and families come back together.

However, when it comes to the restoration of sons and daughters to their parents, we almost always have a happy ending! I can remember the very first Jewish drug addict that came to us out of the ultra-orthodox area of Williamsburg in Brooklyn. In fairness to the young addict's mother, we told her that if her son came into Teen Challenge, and if we were going to help him, he might end up following Jesus Christ.

She answered this way: "Well, my son is dead to me now; if your Jesus can bring him back to life, I'll be very glad for Him to do so." I rejoice to say that her son was "raised from the dead" (spiritually speaking)! Rarely do parents complain about this, regardless of their religious beliefs or unbelief. Praise God, the new birth in Christ Jesus means *new beginnings*—in the home, in the marriage, and in the family!

Chapter 9

How Long Will It Last?

I understood why Maria asked me, "But how can I be sure he's going to stay off drugs? *How long will it last?* I've seen him come out of other programs, but he always went back to drugs. What's different this time?"

"Jesus," I said as I smiled, trying to reassure her without sounding too simplistic. Maria was the wife of one of our married residents. Her husband was ready to graduate and he wanted to go back home, but she was understandably reluctant, fearful, and skeptical.

"Listen, Maria," I continued, "I can't guarantee you anything, except that I know your husband has received Christ into his heart. He wants to do God's will now. Making your husband clean, and keeping him clean, is God's job—and I know from experience that God does a good job of keeping those He saves. If your husband keeps his eyes on Jesus, and if he follows through on the things he's been taught, he'll be okay. I think he deserves a chance—another chance."

She finally agreed after many hours of counseling, encouragement, and reassurance from me. I prayed that her husband, the soon-to-be Teen Challenge alumnus, did not let me down.

Maria had asked a question that everyone asks who is close to the drug problem and drug treatment programs. How long will a recovered addict or alcoholic stay clean once he steps outside the protective environment of the treatment program?

I can't speak for other programs or other modalities of treatment. I do know that most programs, whether religious or secular, rarely claim to produce any lasting results. In many cases, long-term recovery is based on ongoing involvement in some form of therapy.

I *can* speak for Teen Challenge. Two documented historical studies have been conducted to track the success of our program in the lives of graduates who have left our centers. Both studies have shown that approximately *70 percent* of all Teen Challenge graduates remain clean from drugs for as many as seven years after graduation! (We're sure that most graduates actually stay clean much longer, but the longest study we have was based on a seven-year follow-up.)

In some ways, it's almost unfair to compare secular drug treatment programs with a spiritually based program that is Christ-centered. God has no failures. In reality, there is a 100-percent guarantee that if an individual follows God's path, and maintains his faith in Jesus Christ, he will never fail or fall down for long. The Lord will be with the individual every step of the way. Of course, not all our graduates remain faithful to Christ, but those who "keep the faith" are *kept* in the faith: "who through faith are shielded by God's power until the coming of the salvation that is ready to be revealed in the last time" (1 Pet. 1:5 NIV).

"*Shielded by the power of God.*" This is the reason there is such a high rate of success among Christian drug program graduates! This not only applies to Teen Challenge—but to hundreds of other fine Christian drug programs around the world. Both of the in-depth studies were based on in-depth interviews of large cross sections of Teen Challenge program graduates. They revealed some astounding facts about the effectiveness of our programs.

The first study was conducted in the mid 1970's, and it correlates perfectly with the second study, completed in 1994. The first study was unique in that the United States government paid for it through a research grant from the National Institute on Drug Abuse (NIDA), a part of what was then the U.S. Department of Health, Education, and Welfare (HEW)!

It was conducted by Dr. Catherine Hess, the former assistant chief of the Cancer Control Program of the U.S. Public Health Service at the time. She was previously the Medical Director for the New York Hospital Methadone Clinic (methadone is a substitute drug for heroin that blocks the addict from getting high and keeps him from getting sick).

When Dr. Hess first heard that we claimed a nearly 70-percent cure rate for our program, her response was, "No way." She contacted us to ask what our follow-up methods were. We told her we came up with our estimated figures through informal contact with our graduates. "No one will take you seriously unless you document your success," she told us. "How do you do that?" we asked.

Her solution was to ask our permission to apply for a government research grant! Dr. Hess submitted a research application seeking funds to study the premise that "induction of a religious component into the treatment of drug addicts" is one aspect that produces the large success rate we had claimed for our program. (Privately, she admitted she was setting out to prove our figures wrong.)

I was amazed when Dr. Hess told me she had received a $200,000 government grant for the study! How could she get such funds just for a research project when it was impossible for any "religion-based" drug treatment program to get government funds for rehabilitation work?

Dr. Hess conducted the study with extra care to avoid any bias either for or against Teen Challenge. The interviewers for the study were so carefully selected that *none of them were born-again Christians* who might slant their interview to find the best possible data! Urine samples were taken from the 186 persons studied, and the samples were submitted to laboratory analysis to search for traces of drugs in their systems at the time of the interview.

The interviewers had some interesting experiences with some of the graduates. Each interview took several hours to complete. On one report, the researcher wrote in big, bold letters, "WOW." I can only guess at the meaning. The graduate must have given his full-blown testimony of what Christ had done for him. When the study was finally concluded, the results clearly revealed the phenomenal success of the Teen Challenge drug rehabilitation program:

- 67 percent of the graduates in the study were drug free seven years after leaving the program (verified by urinalysis). The Teen Challenge definition of "drug free" means abstaining from all use of narcotics, marijuana, alcohol, and cigarettes.

- 72 percent of the Teen Challenge graduates continued their education after leaving (earned their G.E.D., or pursued college education).

- 75 percent indicated they were employed at the time of the interview. Of those currently employed, 58 percent had been on their present job for over a year.

- 87.5 percent of the graduates required no additional drug program treatment after leaving, although 90 percent considered themselves addicted to drugs before entering Teen Challenge.

- 67 percent were regular church attendees, with 58 percent involved in some form of church work.

- 92 percent reported good to excellent health.

This was a great encouragement to those of us who had pioneered the Christ-centered approach to drug rehabilitation. It was also, as far as I know, the first time the United States government had paid to prove what the power of God was able to do!

Perhaps the most amazing result of the study was that Dr. Hess, "the skeptic," became a *believer* in Teen Challenge! In her report to NIDA, she wrote:

"I wish to admit that, where Teen Challenge viewed me as their most severe and doubting critic, *the conversion has taken place* ... The findings of this program have renewed my belief that there must be significant answers somewhere, if we can only unlock the door for the majority of drug abusers—not just a few.

"I am led, more and more, to the realization that the addict's psychological dependence is far greater than his physiological dependence. That is why Teen Challenge exists as such a unique and successful rehabilitation center. It is basically a spiritual center. Perhaps we desperately need each other's philosophy."

The original grant proposal sought additional funds for further study of Teen Challenge as a "spiritual modality." The government did not approve the second part of the project despite the success of the first study—or perhaps *because* its favorable results embarrassed the government *for funding so many programs with little-to-no results.*

A second study of Teen Challenge was undertaken by our local center based in Chattanooga, Tennessee. Absolutely no government funds were provided for this study. It was conducted by Dr. Roger Thompson, head of the Criminal Justice Department at the University of Tennessee at Chattanooga.

The survey of alumni was begun in the summer of 1992 and completed in the fall of 1994. The researchers surveyed men who had spent four to six months in the Chattanooga program and then transferred to one of two "second-phase" Teen Challenge facilities in Cape Girardeau, Missouri, or the farm in Rehrersburg, Pennsylvania.

A total of 213 alumni from a 13-year period (1979–1991) were included in the study. The survey examined a number of issues, including the individuals' status concerning a continued drug-free lifestyle, employment, legal status, education, and church attendance. The results of Dr. Thompson's research produced the following findings:

- 72 percent of the respondents had undergone drug treatment prior to entering Teen Challenge, but 88 percent had no additional drug treatment since Teen Challenge.

- 60 percent continued their education upon completion of the program.

- 60 percent were either under the jurisdiction of the court and subject to community supervision, or had charges pending when they entered Teen Challenge. At the time of the interview, 76 percent were free of legal interference.

- 76 percent of the alumni studied attended church regularly, and 60 percent became members of local churches.

- 60 percent indicated that their relationship with family was categorized as being good in comparison to fair or poor or no change, as prior to their Teen Challenge experience.

- 92 percent of the respondents claimed that Teen Challenge had a great impact on their life.

Although all the percentages noted above are good, the one statistic that really counts with us is the status of a graduate's ongoing relationship with Jesus Christ. In the Chattanooga study, 80 percent of the alumni credited developing a personal relationship with Jesus Christ as a major influence in helping them stay off drugs!

When this research is translated into real people, the figures come alive in ways that percentages and data cannot describe or equal. Consider just this small sampling of the walking, talking miracles I like to call "The Teen Challenge 'Hall of the Redeemed'!"

David Fogg: Burbank, California; real estate agent.

I came from a Christian home and family. At the age of 15, my girlfriend at the time introduced me to cocaine. That became my life all through high school. After that I began freebasing crack cocaine.

The next seven years of my life were a blur of robberies and drugs to keep myself going. I spent a lot of time in jail, and I even tried five different rehab centers. I became a street-level transient and a real liability to my parents. Life had no more options available to me. Suicide was my only way out.

My Christian father came to visit me one day in the park where I existed. And he convinced me to try to quit drugs "just one more time."

He had heard about a place called Teen Challenge. Maybe if I tried "one more time" to kick my drug habit, just maybe I could do it. Wanting to please my father, I finally went to Teen Challenge. God didn't just change my life there, He gave me a new life!

I am a real estate agent now, and I recently became a top salesman in our area. I'm on the Board of Directors of the local real estate organization, and I actively participate in Overcomers Outreach. I am married to a lovely Christian woman (also an ex-addict), and we will soon purchase our first new home. I thank God every day for allowing me to try "just one more time" to salvage a worthless, degrading life.

Jan Barendse: Amsterdam, Holland; pastor of the oldest Pentecostal church in Europe; member of the Board of Directors of EurAsia Teen Challenge and Teen Challenge International.

As a child in Amsterdam, Holland, I received religious education early, and I was constantly aware of the presence of God in my life. I dreamed of one day working on the mission field. During my teen years, however, I began to lose the ideals of my childhood and became embittered toward the Church. Today's reality did not correspond with the original ideals of Christianity. After several bitter arguments with my parents over my radical ideas, I left home.

I spent my free time in radical social groups, studying Marxism, and doing trade union work. After a few years, I realized I was disappointed even with these things because of the big gap between the ideals of the people and their lives. I became frustrated and cynical. As a result of depression, I suffered from insomnia: so I began to read everything I could find, hoping to fall asleep.

One evening I read **The Robe**, by Lloyd Douglas. This book impressed me so much that I began to read the Book of Acts in the New

Testament to learn more about the lives of Christians in the first century. I was full of questions. What was a Christian in the Book of Acts like? Where was the source of his strength? What was the secret of his enthusiasm?

One day I was riding my motorcycle through the middle of town when I saw a big tent with a banner that said, "Bread for the Heart." It was a Teen Challenge Outreach. The banner's message caught my attention because of the great emptiness I felt in my heart. In fact, I had planned to commit suicide that night. I stood at the entrance of the tent and watched the people in fascination. I recognized them—they were the people described in the Book of Acts! They had strength, enthusiasm, and happiness. When the meeting was over, a man invited me to come in and asked my opinion of the meeting. I told him I was totally convinced that I needed God in my life, and that I was a sinner who needed forgiveness...

After we talked for a few minutes I followed him toward a small prayer room behind the tent. As soon as I knelt down, a deep awareness of God's presence came over me. I spontaneously began to pray aloud, asking God to forgive my sins. The love of God so overpowered me that all my bitterness, hate, and loneliness disappeared. Three days after my conversion, the Lord called me to serve Him. I knew that moment that I needed to be baptized and go to Bible school.

I went to my new pastor and told him of my decision. At his home, I met Howard Foltz, director of Teen Challenge. He happened to have with him an application form for the Dutch Pentecostal Bible School in Den Haag, and he helped me fill it out. One question on the application asked which ministry I felt led by God to work with. When I told Brother Foltz that I felt called to help troubled youth, he told me that was what Teen Challenge was all about! From that very moment, I was recruited into the "Teen Challenge Army."

Jan later became the director of the first Teen Challenge program in Harlem, Holland; then he became a leader in training others, traveling throughout Europe. He eventually returned to his home country to pastor a historical Pentecostal church. During a visit in 1994, Jan showed me the guest book in his church that had been signed by famous people from the Pentecostal movement, such as Louis Petrii, Smith Wigglesworth, Marie Brown and her husband of Glad Tiding Tabernacle in New York City, and many more.

As I read the list of heroes of the faith from early in this century, I turned to Jan and said, "God has a sense of humor, Jan. To think that a former hippie and Teen Challenge convert from off the streets of Holland is now the pastor of such a historical and highly regarded church, is truly a remarkable thing." Jan is anything but traditional, yet he is loved and respected by his congregation. No one would ever be able to tell that Jan is a product of Teen Challenge unless it was pointed out to them, since his life now is such a contrast from the life of the troubled, radical, rebellious past he once lived.

Steve Hill: Lindale, Texas; Assemblies of God missionary evangelist; served in Argentina; has planted churches in South America and the former Soviet Union; instrumental in opening Teen Challenge in Minsk, Belarus.

At age 13, I was smoking tobacco and marijuana, and even tripping on pills. Those drugs changed my whole way of thinking. I found that the bottle, joint, or pill could temporarily eradicate the guilt, eliminate the confusion, and deliver me from my feelings of isolation. I knew that using the needle would mean physical addiction—and that addiction meant sickness, pain, and probable death—I even wondered why anyone would do it. Still, it meant getting "higher" and "freer"—and I was desperate for some new high, some new meaning, anything! In the end, the voice of self said, "Go ahead. Go along with the others. Just be careful. You can control it. You won't get addicted."

As I melted morphine into a spoon and drew it into the needle, the last hint of conscience warned, "This will mean destruction to you." But it was too late. The needle pressed against my skin. No one else was making me do it. The evil voice had become me. I said, "Go ahead. Push that needle in." As the blood from the puncture dripped off my arm, my mind made its foggy, hazy way into oblivion. My last thoughts were, "Steve, you are now a full-fledged drug addict. You've become nothing...nothing...nothing." Darkness came, and it became my life—gross darkness and oblivion was my only peace. There was no such thing as controlling my addiction: I lived for the next fix...

Eventually my mind and body were burned out. Suicide became more and more appealing. The thoughts of death and the ultimate escape filled my mind. Then came that fateful Saturday morning on October 25th, 1975, when the death angel visited me to take me to my eternal destiny. For four days, from Saturday to Tuesday, convulsions racked my body while the dark cloud of death hovered over my mind and my life. Day and night, Mom was there to hold my hand. But only a power greater than both of us enabled me to live through those hellish days and nights.

On Tuesday morning, October 28th, at 10:50 a.m., a knock came on the door as I lay in my helpless condition. I didn't want to see anyone, yet the young man outside my room had just moved into our city, and he had tried to reach out to me before.

Here was someone offering hope! Still, I was not about to play religious games. He would have to overcome my doubts and unbelief. I protested, "I didn't ever believe in Jesus. I have never prayed to a god in my life. How do I know this Jesus is alive?" My visitor said, "Steve, you are going to have to trust me in this. Jesus is here in this room, and He'll touch your life if you'll just cry out to Him. You don't need to say a fancy prayer. God knows your heart. Just cry out the name, Jesus! Jesus!"

The very sound of that name again and again seemed to bring hope from nowhere! The confusion and fear faded slowly as I looked to the ceiling and began to utter that name with my own lips—"Jesus, Jesus, Jesus, Jesus." Then it happened! A peace and a warmth such as I never felt before filled my body. This power rushed in like a river and took command of everything! I kept crying out His name louder and louder: "Jesus! Jesus! Jesus!!" The more I said it, the greater was my deliverance. The convulsions stopped, the evil presence vanished, and the pulsating walls in my room stood still!

Almost immediately, I felt another presence in the room—this one was beautiful and divine. My visitor friend didn't need to tell me what had happened. It was crystal clear—I had just received the gift of new life by Jesus Christ. He had set me free—*completely* free! For so many years, I had lived in total darkness and bondage to sin. My guilt and sin covered me like a heavy blanket. The testimony of God's Word declared, "Though your sins be as scarlet, they shall be as white as snow; though they be red like crimson, they shall be as wool." [Isaiah 1:18b] Now those words were my testimony too.[1]

Steve has been clean and delivered from drugs, and been serving the Lord now for more than 20 years.

Robert Lloyd: Long Island, New York; Executive Director of Long Island Citizens for Community Values (an organization working to reduce sexual violence by eliminating pornography).

My hard-working parents loved me, but like most young people who don't obey their parents, I ended up in trouble and caused my parents a lot of grief. At the age of 16, I went to jail on a gun charge. At the age of 18, I went to jail again for assault. By age 21, I was dealing drugs as a street hustler. I liked the fast life, the cars, and the money—lots of it.

After living that life for many years, I eventually was arrested for selling narcotics and sentenced under the "Rockefeller law" to "one year-to-life" in prison. In the pen, I became a popular "king pin" by dealing in contraband, and homemade wine, and because I had the only Playboy and Penthouse magazine subscriptions. You'd think I would have learned some lessons by then, but I didn't learn anything. I liked the lifestyle I was in, and prison was like a "College of Criminals"—I learned how to become a better criminal!

Dianne Jack, the sister of a very close friend from high school, came to visit me in prison. She had been a heroin addict, but she had found the Lord, and she witnessed to me. Just to be nice to her as an old friend, I said "Yeah, yeah," but I wasn't interested. Miraculously, I was released from prison and given "life on parole." Within a week I was back in business with my reassembled drug and street hustling crew, but Dianne didn't give up! Finally she convinced me to go to church with her. I liked the meeting, and what I heard. I even raised my hand for salvation, but nothing really changed—I liked my lifestyle too much. I still convinced Dianne that I had given up the old life, and we got married.

I was still hard. My partner got shot and died, and still I didn't wake up. Another friend from the drug world got killed, but it didn't affect me. I wanted what I wanted, and I did it. Then my wife left me, and I went crazy and wild. I wanted her back, and I knew I'd have to change to get her. God used that to convict me. I began staying at home, and I even got a job and worked. That was real hard. I began going to a church among some very caring and righteous people who loved me and wanted to help me. But still I had one foot in hell and one in the church.

I began to cry out to God, "I need help. I can't stop this lifestyle. I can't do this." I realized I had no control over my drug habit; it was controlling me. One day while going to work, I pulled to the side of the road at six o'clock in the morning and prayed, "Lord, I'm tired of living a double life. If You're real, make a way for me."

Soon after this, my pastor said, "Robert, we found a place where you can get help—it's called Teen Challenge." I said, "I'm not going there. I'm over 30 years old. I'm not going to a place with a bunch of teenagers!" They explained it was for people my age as well, but I still didn't want to go. They kept talking about it and finally I was open to it, but still not sure. I prayed, "Lord, if this is for me, then show me."

A visitor came to speak in our little church, and in the midst of his talk he began talking about his visit to a Teen Challenge Center outside New York City, and how he saw a bunch of ex-cons, dope-users, and fellows you would normally be afraid to even speak to—had their hands up praising God. When he said the place was "Teen Challenge," immediately I thought, "This is a setup. My wife and pastor told this man to say those things just to try and convince me, but I'm not going to fall for it!"

I was so upset that I said to myself, "When this guy comes down from off the platform, I'm going to grab him by the neck and he's going to tell me the truth." Finally he came down and I stopped him before he could do anything. He told me, "Listen, brother, I have no idea why I said that. It just came to my mind as I was preaching. The Lord put that on my heart." That settled it for me—I was going to Teen Challenge in Brooklyn.

I was sent to the upstate New York facility they had at the time, and there I really found a personal relationship with Jesus Christ. After graduation, I wanted to go to Bible school, but that was not feasible because my five daughters were unsaved and running wild back home. I had to zero in on them. I thank God I obeyed the Lord because four of my daughters are saved and serving the Lord today, and the fifth one is on her way.

Wolfgang Mueller: Niederhausen, Germany; business accountant; mayor candidate for his local village.

Wolfgang was invited by a Teen Challenge worker to visit the Teen Challenge coffee house in Wiesbaden, Germany, while he was on his way home from an amateur rock group practice session. At 16, Wolfgang belonged to a gang, most of whom smoked hashish and marijuana, and although he refused to take drugs, he smoked and drank as heavily as the others. Like most teenagers, his main interest in life was to have a good time, so he was not interested in the coffee house. But the invitation proved to be the turning point in his life.

Shortly after the encounter with the Teen Challenge worker, Wolfgang discovered that another member of his rock group had been invited to the coffee house too. They discussed this coincidence and decided to check it out when they had nothing else to do. That opportunity arrived several months later.

Wolfgang and his friends had planned to attend a rock concert, but when they reached the music hall, they couldn't afford the tickets. Disconsolate, they stood outside discussing what they could do when

Wolfgang suddenly realized they were not far from the coffee house. He tried to persuade the others to go there, but only his best friend agreed to accompany him.

On the way, Wolfgang said to his friend, "I'm going to ask those people questions they won't be able to answer. When we leave tonight, they will no longer believe what they think they believe now." He was convinced no one could answer his questions, such as, "What is the reason for living?" and "Why do we exist in the way we do?" He also had many scientific and pseudo-scientific questions about evolution and creation. Wolfgang was looking forward to a stimulating discussion.

Upon reaching the coffee house, the two sat down at a table. A worker sat down across from them and a conversation began. Wolfgang was amazed when the worker was able to answer all his questions. He had never believed people really could know why they exist, who made them, or who God is. The idea of having a personal contact with God was new to Wolfgang. That night, he became impressed by what he heard and saw in the lives of the workers.

Wolfgang and his friend returned the following evening and spoke to the same worker. They were astonished at his patience as he answered the same questions over and over again, with no sign of frustration. By the end of the evening, Wolfgang knew he needed to repent and turn his life over to Christ. However, when he was asked to go to the prayer room, he suddenly became anxious and said he had to leave immediately to catch the last bus home.

On the bus, he suggested to his friend that they find out if prayer really worked, "We'll ask God to send sparks of light into a dark room when we pray." Sitting in the darkness that night, Wolfgang was disappointed when nothing supernatural happened in answer to his prayer. The next weekend, Wolfgang and his friend returned again to complain that prayer "doesn't work." The worker carefully repeated the way of salvation, and again Wolfgang was impressed with the worker's patience—especially since he was being critical and doubtful. Before the end of the evening, Wolfgang and his friend accepted Christ into their lives. "I was a changed person from that time on," Wolfgang said.

After a period of discipleship, Wolfgang was baptized in water and in the Holy Spirit. He began ministering in the coffee house, reaching out to other young people trapped in defeating lifestyles. He worked there for five years part-time and eventually became a full-time staff member, and was director of Teen Challenge in Germany for a number of years.

Jimmy Jack: Centereach, Long Island, New York; Executive Director of Long Island Teen Challenge; pastor of Freedom Chapel, Amityville, New York.

In the nearly 36 years I've worked with substance abusers, I have *never* seen a family more devastated by drugs and alcohol than the Jack family! Nor have I ever seen more miracles take place in one family! All seven of the Jack children became either hardcore addicts or alcoholics! Both parents, Adelle and Hugh, were substance abusers. Adelle was addicted to pills, and Hugh was an alcoholic. Four of their children also married drug addicts, and the family took in another unofficial adoptee and official heroin addict named Billy. *Thus, a total of 14 members of the Jack family were addicts!*

Jimmy Jack spent five years on hard drugs. He came from a middle-class family. His father was a district high school athletic director. Jimmy loved sports—and played hard at it, but drugs interrupted this. He was kicked off the varsity high school basketball team after being arrested for a drug-related burglary. Jimmy and his best friend Billy (who the family treated as their own son) became drug partners—shooting $100 a day each in heroin and cocaine, and using alcohol. This is his story.

Billy and I tried many different programs to get free from this torment. We'd enter detox programs together, pretending we did not know each other because friends are not permitted in the same program. We always abused the programs and the patients who were trying to get their lives together. We were hopeless; living out of cars or in friends' homes; never able to keep a job or an apartment.

I was desperate for money so I asked my sister Dianne to lend me $200. She'd been a heroin addict and became a Christian [her husband Robert Lloyd's testimony is mentioned earlier] and was always praying for me. She told me she knew one day I'd be serving the Lord. When I asked her for the money, Dianne said, "Sure, come down to my church and I'll give it to you there." I knew she had an ulterior motive.

I went and got there at the end of the service, when everyone was praying. My sister said, "Let us pray for you first, Jim, and then I'll give you the money." Well, she had the money, so I prayed. I was nervous, but with a sincere heart I asked the Lord to please help me because I knew I was dying. I remember specifically saying, "**Lord, if You are real, show me!**"

A few days later Billy and I were in the lower East Side of Manhattan, New York, in my van. I snorted one bag of heroin, and I held Billy's arm as he shot three bags into his vein. When I let go of his arm, Billy overdosed and fell out of the van. I grabbed him and gave him mouth-to-mouth resuscitation, but he did not respond. I tried everything that I had learned in the streets to keep Billy from overdosing, but nothing worked. He turned blue and life left him. I began crying hysterically. I loved Billy closer than a brother. The only thing left to do was cry out to God.

Out of nowhere an ambulance showed up. They told me to pick Billy up and place him in the van. It took all the strength I had. They began to shoot him with neutralizers and give him oxygen, but still there was no response. They were shaking their heads, saying, "It's too late! It's too late." I shouted to the paramedics, "You keep working on him!" while I went to the side of my van and cried out to God, "Please save Billy! If You do, I promise I'll give my life to You." When I finished praying, Billy's heart suddenly began to beat, and he woke up!

The Lord instantly brought me back in my mind to the church service with my sister Dianne, when I had asked God to show me that He was real. He did—on the streets of Manhattan. He spared Billy's life, yet I did not live up to my promise—I kept getting high. I knew God had created a miracle by saving Billy. Fear came over me that I was not fulfilling my promise. A couple of weeks later, Billy was stabbed in the chest over a drug deal. I got him out of the hospital, and we both agreed to go to Dianne's church and get prayer.

We walked down the aisle together with the scent of death hovering over us. I'd lost my van, my work tools, everything was lost but my girlfriend, Miriam—she stuck by me. A few weeks later, my life of addiction and misery ended and a new life began—in a bar on skid row! I was twisted on drugs, and I began acting weird and incoherent. I was carrying a large screwdriver, and I was out to hurt someone—anyone who got in my way. I was angry at myself and my situation, and I was convicted by the fact I had not fulfilled my promise to God to stop using drugs.

In this "danger zone" of my drug craze, God sent an angel in the form of an old friend named George. "Come on, Jim—don't do something stupid now," he warned me. Then he grabbed me, and held on to me while he called my sister, Dianne. She got in her car, drove to the bar, picked me up, and delivered me personally to the Brooklyn Teen Challenge Center!

I woke up the next day smelling like a garbage pail. But I asked Jesus to enter this filthy person, and He did! I knew then and there that I was healed—and needed never to go back to drugs again. Three months later, Miriam and I were married, and we entered the Teen Challenge program together.

The actual number of Teen Challenge ministry converts worldwide, including both the outreach programs and the residential centers, would fill numerous school yearbook volumes! Some of the conversions are more dramatic than others—but they all have one thing in common: They provide living proof that "the cross is still mightier than the switchblade"! Yes, the cross is mightier than the narcotic needle and drug substance— no matter what form it comes in or how powerfully it once controlled the lives of those who entered a Teen Challenge Center.

Whether it was Nicky Cruz over 35 years ago in Brooklyn, or Wolfgang in Germany; whether it was Jan in Holland or David in Burbank, California; everyone who walks into one of the hundreds of centers operating 24 hours a day, year in and year out, around the world—discovers that Teen Challenge is still in the business of recycling broken people!

Endnotes

1. Taken from *Stone Cold Heart* by Steve Hill. Published by Together in the Harvest Publications, P.O. Box 2050, Lindale, Texas 75771. Copyright 1995. Used by permission of author.

Chapter 10

Jesus "Saves": The Economics of Salvation

Every person who graduates from "God's Mountain," the Teen Challenge rehabilitation and discipleship farm in Rehrersburg, Pennsylvania, is preparing to *show what great things God hath done*"! The same miracle is happening in other long-term Teen Challenge rehabilitation programs in numerous locations around the United States and the world.

These graduates have completed the four different phases of the Teen Challenge program, walking them through their "new birth" to their final "reentry" into society. Phase One involves outreach evangelism. Phase Two is called "Induction," and it lasts from three to six months. Phase Three is "Basic Training," which runs for an additional six to nine months, and Phase Four is the reentry stage. Some Teen Challenge Centers do all four phases, while many smaller centers specialize in one or two of the phases. Overseas Teen Challenge Centers keep their residents at one location for the duration of their rehabilitation.

We train the residents in our long-term facilities to go back home to their parents, spouses, and families *free of their addictions* and *full of the Spirit of God.* If they have no family, we link them with sponsors who will take them under their wings as they reenter society.

Some graduates go on to further their education in Bible institutes, liberal arts colleges, or other training schools. Many of these Teen Challenge graduates enter the ministry as pastors, evangelists, missionaries, teachers, or other church or parachurch workers! On special occasions, we hold "homecoming" celebrations for our graduates, when the modern "lepers" of our society, as it were, return and give thanks to God for their healing!

At one of these homecoming celebrations, I looked at the faces of hundreds of "salvaged" men and women, and the Holy Spirit suddenly spoke to me about "the economics of salvation." The fact that hundreds of men and women were no longer in sin and costly drug addiction means that *Teen Challenge is saving the U.S. taxpayers money—lots of money!*

The New York Times reported that by 1992, the United States had poured nearly $70 billion into fighting drugs over the previous 20 years—with little or no success! This doesn't include costs for treatment or prevention. It only reflects the cost for law enforcement in dealing with the drug problem, particularly the interception of drugs prior to or at an entry point into the country.[1]

In the fiscal year of 1996, the U.S. budget projected spending $14.6 billion for drug abuse control—10 percent more than in 1995; $2.8 billion for drug treatment delivery—$180 million more than in 1995; and $7.2 billion for criminal justice expenses related to drug problems![2]

Is there any government agency that does not get anti-drug money? Apparently not. Even the U.S. Information Agency will get over $10.1 million to sponsor programs abroad—to explain U.S. drug control policies to foreign governments! "Boot camps" are new and innovative prison programs that provide rigorous discipline, physical conditioning, job training, counseling, and education for convicted drug offenders. Construction of new "boot camps" scheduled to open in 1996 will cost $500 million dollars. Yet another $150 million will go to expand and improve drug courts—a nearly fivefold increase over 1995![3]

The drug problem is a staggering financial drain on the economy, and on the weary taxpayer in particular! Those drug offenders who are not helped through the government's prevention or treatment programs will end up in prison—which is yet another costly item!

There is a solution! There is a proven way to save on some of this cost. Teen Challenge is doing it. Jesus Christ is doing it. Every time a drug addict finds Christ and returns to society "free indeed," the financial savings to the government and taxpayer adds up quickly.

For example, it costs taxpayers approximately $20,000 to incarcerate one prisoner for one year. Using a base of just 100 Teen Challenge rehabilitation program graduates to calculate figures, let us assume these graduates were *not* saved, and were still on drugs. If each of these individuals spent an average of two or more years in prison in their lifetimes (believe me, this is a *conservative estimate!*), the cost to you and me as taxpayers to incarcerate, guard, clothe, and feed these unrehabilitated drug addicts would be a total of *4 million dollars* in their lifetimes!

Yes, it is safe to say, "Jesus saves." That is an economic statement as well as a spiritual reality!

Let's carry the analogy further. By conservative estimates, the average drug addict spends an average of $25 per day supporting his habit. That amounts to $9,125 dollars per year—*most of which is stolen from the public* in some form or another.

Let us assume again that our 100 graduates have *not* been saved and delivered from drugs by the power of God. In one year alone, this group would spend $912,500 to support their habits by taking money out of the pockets of hard-working Americans who *don't* take drugs. In reality, the actual drug cost for 100 addicts would cost millions of dollars!

Consider this: Twenty-five hundred young people go through Teen Challenge during a year's time. If their rehabilitation cost was borne by the taxpayer—*it would cost approximately 55 million dollars for the year!* However, neither the United States government or the taxpayer has to pay out this 55 million dollars! This cost is paid for completely by the faithful gifts and donations of concerned Christians!

Again, it is safe to say that "Jesus saves!" He saves us economically as well as through spiritual and moral salvation.

According to *The Economist*, "The economic cost of America's drug habit is, at a guess, somewhere between $50 billion and $100 billion a year."[4] Did you notice that the figures refer to "billions," not merely millions of dollars?!

There are countless other costs that have not been figured into this picture, such as cost of the court trials for addicts who have been arrested and accused of a crime. There are also mountains of hospital costs for addicts and substance abusers admitted for detoxification, or for treatment of physical problems brought on by drug addiction or alcohol abuse. These services are provided free of cost to the abuser—because it is paid for out of your pockets and mine!

Our government's welfare system makes it very easy for addicts to collect welfare and other benefits, which they use to support their habit. One report stated: "Junkies and alcoholics are drawing monthly disability checks for their drug habits—some even while in jail—under a little-known Social Security program that has grown by 300 percent in California over the past three years."[5]

Long before Congress and the President decided to "change the welfare system as we know it," Teen Challenge had been dismantling the destructive "welfare mentality" for more than three decades—one case at a time! We have always taught our residents in the program, "If a man will not work, he will not eat!" That is right out of the Bible. (See Second Thessalonians 3:10.)

We were able to calculate the number of persons who were taken off of welfare as a result of graduating from Teen Challenge and serving the Lord this way: If 30 percent of our current residents were on welfare before coming into a center, that would amount to 750 people (based on the approximately 2,500 residents in a Teen Challenge Center on any given day).

If each of these 750 residents would normally receive $9,600 in welfare support in one year (which is a very low figure for most urban areas), then the Teen Challenge rehabilitation programs singlehandedly save the federal government (and U.S. taxpayers) $7.2 million dollars in welfare costs alone each year! This amounts to a savings of $36 million dollars over a five-year period—assuming our pool of graduates doesn't grow and multiply each year (which it does!).

This is yet another example proving that "Jesus saves" taxpayers money every time a soul is saved—not only in the United States, but in every country where the government is expected to provide financial and material support to drug addicts, substance abusers, and their families.

By our conservative estimates, Teen Challenge saves the U.S. taxpayers upwards of $62.2 million each year through the drug rehabilitation services it provides, and the number of its graduates who no longer seek welfare support. This doesn't include the savings enjoyed in reduced prison expenses and crime prevention when addicts are forever rescued from the street and delivered from the drug world!

I told Teen Challenge graduates at one homecoming celebration, "I think I'm going to do a line-by-line item savings estimate of what Jesus Christ and Teen

Challenge have saved the United States government. I think I should send the President a bill for Jesus' services!" The graduates clapped and hollered their approval.

When I think of the efforts of some liberals and humanists to deny tax-exempt status to the Church, and other Christian organizations like ours (and there has been talk of this for sure), I want them to meet the two to five percent of the people in evangelical churches who once lived in gross sin. They once drained the government treasury to take care of problems resulting from their sin!

I want them to count the number of people in church who no longer divorce their wives, waste their employer's money through lost job time because of alcohol abuse, or run up hospital costs because they abuse their bodies with cigarettes, pills, legal and illegal drugs, or end up in prison! Teen Challenge is not the only place where addicts are cured—tens of thousands are saved in local churches every year, and as a result, live drug- and alcohol-free lives! Then I'd like to take these same unbelievers into one of our many Teen Challenge Centers and explain the economics of salvation, as well as the eternal values of salvation in Jesus Christ.

I would especially like to take certain bureaucrats from the state of Texas on a nationwide tour of our rehabilitation centers. Someone in the "Program Compliance Division" of the Texas Commission of Alcohol and Drug Abuse ruled that our San Antonio Teen Challenge branch should be *shut down* for not complying with some of their nit-picking standards (such as failure to follow its directive for keeping certain personnel files on clients, and not having "non-slip surfaces" on the stairs)!

A deeper and more serious problem lies behind this needless harassment: the state does not recognize *religious conversion* as a proper means of rehabilitating drug addicts and alcoholics! Nor does it recognize the qualifications of the Teen Challenge staff as being of sufficient "professional" quality. (Never mind that our staff is *successful*, while their "professionally" staffed programs fail miserably year after year at considerable taxpayer expense!)

The prestigious *Wall Street Journal* reported our battle with the Texas bureaucracy in a piece entitled, "Addicted to Bureaucracy." The article stated:

"For three decades, conform-or-die bureaucrats have told drug treatment groups to rely on licensed professional counselors with theoretical training, rather than the ex-addicts and reformed alcoholics who lead many of the Teen Challenge chapters. In the past, religious-based groups facing state pressure have either buckled or lowered their profile. But Teen Challenge is holding firm."[6]

The article goes on to say:

"Teen Challenge may lack counselors with fancy degrees, but it has the advantage of a national quality-control system, with local members required by the organization to conform to 98 standards dealing with everything from financial accountability to cleanliness...Unfortunately, the Texas bureaucracy cares only about means, not ends. 'Outcomes and outputs are not an issue with us,' stated one of the bureaucrats from the Commission on Alcohol and Drug Abuse. He also sent a blunt letter to Teen Challenge stating that if they did not close down, it would be committing a Class A misdemeanor (punishable by up to a year in jail, a fine of up to $4,000, or both, with each day Teen Challenge is open counting as a separate offense)."[7]

None of this caused our people to bow down to this Caesar of the Southwest. Instead, a public rally was held in front of the Alamo with 325 people standing (many of them converted addicts) in the midday sun for two hours, singing gospel hymns and carrying placards saying: "Because of Jesus I am No Longer a Debt to the State of Texas" and "Once a Burden, Now a Taxpayer." *The Wall Street Journal* printed the results of the rally: "But the resolve of state bureaucrats did not melt in the 95-degree heat. They stuck to their demands that the program that has produced such success close down...."[8]

The saga of our modern "Battle of the Alamo" is still unfolding and unfinished. Ultimately we know that God's power, and a methodology based on biblical principles, will prevail—in spite of such challenges from state agencies.

The "economics of salvation" is also revealed in the ordinary everyday life of a Teen Challenge graduate who has reentered society. Eddie immediately comes to my mind. He came back to visit me shortly after he left the program. He'd gotten a job and he wanted to tell me about it—and show me something that was *very special*.

I can still see his smile as he pulled out a piece of paper. It was his paycheck stub. "Look at this, Brother Don," Eddie said as he proudly held it up for me to see. He watched for my reaction, and apparently he thought I should have made more of it than I did.

"Maybe this does not impress you. I know you've had a lot of rewards in your life, and a lot of accomplishments. But you need to understand something!" Eddie said as he began to lecture me. "This paycheck stub represents *the first legitimate money* I've ever made in my life! I never worked before—I always stole for my money. I now *earn* a living—and I'm proud of it!"

When he explained it in those terms, I congratulated him with the level of excitement and appreciation that better matched the miraculous nature of his achievement. Then Eddie told me about an incident on his job that week.

"Brother Don, I was stocking radios in the shelves...I don't have a fancy job; I'm just a stock boy. Anyway, I was putting the radios on the shelves and singing that little chorus I learned at Teen Challenge, 'Thank You Lord, for saving my soul; Thank You Lord, for making me whole! Thank You Lord, for giving to me, Thy great salvation so full and free!' "

Then Eddie started to laugh, and I looked at him and smiled, wondering what the punch line was. "As I was singing it I began to laugh," Eddie continued. "The thought struck me that my boss should have been thankful for my salvation, because if Jesus had not saved me, those radios would not have been going up on the shelf; they would have been going out the back door. I would have been stealing them!"

Consider the growing percentage of problems caused by drug abuse in American companies: absenteeism—54 percent; accidents—39 percent; increases in medical expenses—39 percent; thefts—36 percent; product or service quality problems—33 percent.[9]

When I think of the economics of salvation, I think of the woman in the Bible who had an "issue of blood." In her desperate search for relief from her problem, she "...had spent *all* her living upon physicians, neither could be healed of any" (Lk. 8:43). That woman was a lot like another class of "incurable victims." Many drug abusers and alcoholics—from the working class as well as the upper-income brackets—pay multiplied thousands of dollars on their own or through insurance policies for therapeutic treatment of their condition in hospitals. However, I have some good news: There is a better way! Jesus has already paid it all. By His death on the cross, the gift of salvation can be received by anyone—free of charge!

Teen Challenge does not charge its residents for their treatment. Our vital ministry to the hurting and helpless is totally funded by concerned Christians who give out of a heart of love for the hurting! Those who are not able to enter a Teen Challenge Center can enter any Bible-believing church and find salvation in

Christ "full and free"! Not only will their soul be saved, but their life will be saved as well.

As the national debt nears five trillion dollars, it is time to consider the economic savings of salvation in Christ Jesus. A spiritual revival in America would have a profound effect on our national debt! I invite federal, state, and local legislators to look closely at Teen Challenge—*it is a microcosm of the "economics of salvation"*!

Endnotes

1. Joseph B. Treaster, "20 Years of War on Drugs and No Victory Yet," *The New York Times* (June 14, 1992), p. 7.

2. CRS Report for Congress, (Congressional Research Service).

3. CRS Report for Congress.

4. *The Economist* (Jan. 21, 1989).

5. "Drug Addicts Draw Pay From Government," April 1, 1992 (Prodigy Services Co.).

6. Marvin Olasky, "Addicted to Bureaucracy," *The Wall Street Journal* (August 15, 1993).

7. Olasky, "Addicted to Bureaucracy."

8. Olasky, "Addicted to Bureaucracy."

9. Hoffman-La Ruche Inc. study of October 1989, reported in *USA Today* (Dec. 7, 1989), p. 1A.

Chapter 11

The Challenge Heard Around the Globe

Ten years after Teen Challenge Centers began springing up throughout the United States, God sent along a man with the burden to reach the drug addicts in *other countries*. Howard Foltz, a former Teen Challenge worker in Houston, Texas, was sent by the Assemblies of God Foreign Missions Department to raise up Teen Challenge in Europe. Thanks to Howard's labors, Holland became the first foreign country to host a Teen Challenge Center.

When Howard came to David and me asking for our support, David gave him two instructions: "First, open a center in one country and use it as a model to show other countries what this ministry is. Then establish a training center where people from other countries can come to learn how to do street outreach, how to reach troubled youth, and to learn the principles by which Teen Challenge operates."

When Howard moved into Holland, God began to pour out His Spirit through street evangelism, coffee

157

house ministry, and rehabilitation centers! Within ten years, the second part of the vision was implemented. Howard had managed to put together a dedicated team of American and European training directors and staff members from many nations. This, in turn, birthed the opening of very effective Teen Challenge Centers in many other nations, including Germany, France, Denmark, Italy, and Portugal.

I stayed very close to the work overseas, and tried to help in whatever way I felt was needed. I often introduced the ministry in new countries through rallies, seminars, and other public meetings. In many ways, I felt our work in New York City was more like an overseas ministry, given the various cultures we reached. New York City is an international melting pot of cultures, and after living and working there for so many years, I discovered that I felt very comfortable in my European work for Teen Challenge.

A historic meeting for World Teen Challenge took place in 1994, on the occasion of the twenty-fifth anniversary of the day Howard Foltz established the first Teen Challenge in Europe (the organization is now called EurAsia Teen Challenge; it is directed by Al Perna, Jr., an Assembly of God missionary). I was privileged to be the speaker for the special anniversary celebration, which was held in Belgium.

During that time, I chaired a meeting of directors from around the world. I presented them with the need and challenge to establish an international organization, a "fellowship" of international Teen Challenge Centers. An international organization of some kind was urgently needed to help my brother, David, as well as myself, respond to the growing number of requests for help in starting Teen Challenge programs in countries where no such outreach program exists.

Very soon after the demise of communism in Europe, churches in eastern Europe began making contact with western Europe and the Western nations. One of the things we discovered is that they desperately wanted to reach their troubled youth. They asked if Teen Challenge Centers could be started in their nations and urban areas. The "fall" of the Berlin wall brought new freedoms—and the "freedom to sin" in new ways! The major American companies were not the only ones setting up shop in the key former communist countries—so were the criminals, pornographers, and dope dealers!

One reason the Church in the former Soviet Union and other nations under the old communist alliance were, and still are, asking for the Teen Challenge ministry is because they had all read one book—even though it was not officially approved or available in print under communism. *The Cross and the Switchblade* had even proven that the cross was mightier than the so-called "Iron Curtain" of repressive communism!

In Russia, for example, some believers during the communist era translated and typed out the entire book on thin, rough, typewriter paper and compiled it into a crude manual. One underground church missionary told me, "Don, I saw a copy of the book when I was in Russia. It had been passed around so many times, and read by so many people, that the type was fading and the edges of the paper were worn and torn. The people loved that book!"

When I asked him why it was so popular, he said, "Because it's a modern Book of Acts! It shows the miraculous. It's like reading the twenty-ninth chapter of the Book of Acts!"

One of the first pastors to come to us from a former Soviet satellite nation was Victor Boyesko, from the Ukraine. He spoke in Times Square Church, where I was pastoring with my brother at the time. He said he had sent a letter to President Gorbachev asking for religious freedom for the Church—and he was one of the last pastors arrested before the "Iron Curtain" fell. Boyesko was placed in prison in the city of Lviv, Ukraine, where he lived. He was in solitary confinement for months before he was finally transferred to a regular prison and placed among common criminals.

"I was given a mattress and taken to a prison dormitory where I would have to share a bunk with someone," he explained. "I looked around the room at a group of hard-core criminals, trying to pick out one that didn't look too vicious. I'd asked the Lord not to put me in such a place, but it must have been God's will, for there I was. I decided to share a bunk with the meekest-looking prisoner in the room, thinking it might be safer with him. It turned out he had killed his own mother with an axe. So much for my discernment."

As I looked at this mild-mannered, dignified pastor, I could not imagine a worse contrast between him and the sort of characters with which he was forced to spend years in confinement. "God had a purpose for putting me in such a hell-hole," Pastor Boyesko shared. "I got a burden for those men. And I made a commitment to the Lord that I would try to help those like them in or out of prison."

After the pastor completed his prison sentence, Gorbachev fell from power and the doors for ministry opened wide in ways that were never possible under communism. "One of the first things I desired to do when I went to America was to visit David Wilkerson and ask if he would help us with this ministry," he told our congregation. David turned to me on the platform as we listened to this former underground church pastor share his heart, and said, "Don, let's help this brother. As soon as you can arrange it, go over to his city and help him open a Teen Challenge there."

Months later, I did just that. I discovered that Pastor Boyesko was a hero to the new government leaders. His arrest by the communist regime had been in all the newspapers. Because he had taken a stand for freedom, when freedom finally came to his people, his valiant stand was not forgotten. Now he has friends in high places. I visited with mayors, the state governor, the surgeon general, and other city leaders. Everyone asked, "Please help us reconstruct a new society. Help us with our youth and their problems."

The governor told me, "Our youth have no ideology, and nothing to believe in anymore. There is a moral vacuum in our land. We have many economic and social problems. Please come and set up your program and help the drug addicts and alcoholics."

As I traveled from Moscow to Minkz, in Belurus, and then through the Ukraine, I was totally unprepared for what I saw. The former Soviet Union was, and in many cases still is, in *worse* shape than many Third World countries! Besides their economic problems, alcoholism is raging at epidemic proportions. I wondered, *How can they cope with a drug problem on top of all that?*

When I visited their drug and alcohol treatment center in a local hospital, we were offered an entire wing of the hospital to set up Teen Challenge! I'll never forget the sight of one addict (who became hooked on drugs during the war in Afghanistan, much like American soldiers did in Vietnam). He stands out in my mind, as he lay in his bed staring at me with a forlorn look in his eyes, pleading, "Please send someone to help us!"

"I will, I will," I promised him; then I prayed for the entire ward filled with hopeless drug addicts. Some of the nurses and directors at the hospital were moved to tears, as was I.

I returned to America with a prayer and a job I had to do. Somehow, somewhere, I had to find *someone* to answer this urgent call to the drug addicts of a nation gone bankrupt morally, socially, and economically! My prayer was answered in Jim and Sandy McCann, who were working in the Teen Challenge Center in Washington, D.C. I rejoiced when Jim told me, "I have felt for a long time the Lord wanted Sandy and I to go to some former Soviet country. We didn't know when, or how, but we just knew it was a call from the Lord."

The McCanns answered that call and moved to the Ukraine to learn the language. They hope to open a Teen Challenge Center there soon in the Lord's timing. Meanwhile, the Holy Spirit was also working on behalf of the people in Central Asia, in the capital city of the new Republic of Kazakhstan, Alta Alma, formerly under the control of the defunct Soviet Union. Doug Boyle, a former Teen Challenge worker from Australia, is seeing miracles occur among drug addicts there.

There is something especially remarkable about a Teen Challenge Center being planted in Alta Alma. For more than a thousand years, it has been an important center for the cultivation of *opium*, from which *heroin* is derived! Doug told us, "A sin has been uncovered among the youth of the former U.S.S.R. that is so terrible in its consequences and so enormous in scale, that it threatens the very future of the newly formed national states! It is drug addiction. When *COMICON*—the former Soviet economic trading block—collapsed, the newly independent states turned to the West for help, seeking new ways and new markets to raise capital. They discovered that *selling narcotics* was one of those ways."

Fueled by the chance to make "big bucks," drug trafficking has now become one of the leading industries in Central Asia. The main casualties here, as in the West, are the nation's future, its young people. The most common drug used is "hanka" or "muk." It is produced by crushing the opium poppy seed to release a narcotic resin that is then processed into a paste about the consistency of peanut butter. This is soluble and used for injection. Most users use it as is, but it is often further refined to a white sap that is more popular in big cities like Moscow where there is more money. It is the base for heroin production. "Hanka" sells in Alta Alma for $6 to $8 a gram, but it sells in Tashkent, Uzbekistan, for $1,000 a kilogram!

Doug Boyle shrugged and said, "Who knows what it's worth in Germany? The addicts who came to our Teen Challenge program used an average of two grams a day! One girl, who is now 20, was using seven grams a day, and she started at age 13. Some of our men have used up to an unbelievable ten grams of 'hanka' a day. Many of our clients say 'hanka' was the *first* drug they used! How is this possible? Narcotics are cheap and readily available. Within a 200-meter radius of our center, there are dozens of sellers happy to provide the poison. Marijuana grows by the roadside here (and in our backyard; it is a common garden weed), but just a little further on are the opium fields."

Doug described even more reasons why the ministry of Teen Challenge is so important to this region of the world. "One retired policeman estimated that 70 percent of the young people over the age of ten are using illegal drugs here! I know this sounds impossible, but the testimony of one of our female students paints an even darker picture. She said, 'I started smoking marijuana with my friends at school when I was 11. I later smoked hashish and opium, and I first started shooting narcotics when I was 13. At 17, in my last year at school, there were 30 students in my class—every one of us smoked hashish and marijuana, and 15 of us were shooting hanka as well.' "

In a country where unemployment, alcoholism, and family breakdown is the norm rather than the exception, coupled with the availability of relatively cheap narcotics, and very cheap hashish and marijuana, it is possible that the youth of Central Asia are among the *most severely drug-addicted youth on the face of the earth!*

It is there, in the field of drugs, that some of satan's captives are being set free. The first Teen Challenge Center for Central Asia is introducing a new power in the blood and lives of young people who have polluted their blood with narcotics. Male and female addicts alike are finding Christ for the first time—and most of them are Moslem.

When Murat came to the center in Kazakhstan at the age of 30, he had already been using drugs for 15 years. He said, "The very first time I tried drugs, I died for the first time." He meant that after that first shot of dope, he felt like he ceased to be normal and human. "It cost a lot of money. I used opium (hanka)—taking several shots a day. I was dead, but did not realize it. My parents sent me to the army, and for a time, I was clean. But as soon as I came out of the army, I joined a gang, and we stole cars, stripped them down, and sold the parts. Then one day I had an accident in my parents' car—I was so addicted I lost memory of what I was doing. I lost everything, and tried to commit suicide. My parents called emergency help to resuscitate me. I know God saved me [from death]. I even tried sorcery, trying to get into a trance for a cure."

None of this worked, for Marut went right back to drugs; much to the dismay of his father, a Muslim mullah (clergyman). Murat did not realize it, but his sister had became a born-again Christian at about this time. Through her urging he was brought to the Teen Challenge Center. "There I also became born again, and got a new start in life. I feel like I am 20 years old now, and starting all over."

When Doug Boyle met Murat's Muslim father, the father said to him, "You are a man of God." Doug wanted to be sure the father understood that the program was based on a personal relationship with Jesus Christ. He told Murat's father, "But we are Christians. I am a Christian! Your son has become a Christian." The father's ready answer was: "That's okay! You are a man of God—you gave me back my son." Not even a Muslim, even if he is a mullah, could argue with that kind of salvation and deliverance.

In another part of the world, Teen Challenge is reaching addicts in a very unusual place and in an unusual way. Rodney Hart, a former drug addict and graduate of Teen Challenge, serves in Ascension, Paraguay, as an Assemblies of God missionary. He has opened a home for addicts, but he also runs another division of Teen Challenge—*inside a federal prison*! This unique, full-blown Teen Challenge program operates totally within the prison's walls, and is staffed by converted prisoners who were reached through Rodney and Teen Challenge!

When he was first invited to preach in the prison, Rodney shared his own testimony and preached, and many inmates got saved. Then he returned to disciple them. One by one, prisoner by prisoner, these men began to show evidence of a changed life. The prison guards, as well as the warden, noticed that the Teen Challenge converts no longer were rebellious, or gave the guards problems, or even smoked. They revolutionized the prison from within!

The warden quickly saw the need for a regular chapel in which the growing Christian population could meet (they did not have one at that point, since prison conditions in that country are very bleak). He granted permission for Rodney to build a chapel, and through the efforts of the Brethren Church, funds were given and a chapel was constructed.

One day, the warden invited Rodney in to see him—and presented him with an unprecedented challenge, even for an organization that has the word "challenge" in its very name! "I see the good work you are doing, Rev. Hart," the warden said. "How would you like to build a Teen Challenge Center right on our property? You can either take one of our old buildings and fix it up, or have some of the land and build a whole new facility. It will be your Teen Challenge Center."

Rodney accepted the challenge, and today this project is currently in development, waiting for further funding. Only God could do this: raise up a center for inmates, run by converted inmates—a full-fledged Teen Challenge program right on the prison grounds!

There is one particular Teen Challenge Center that may well be faced with the greatest need and challenge of any place on the face of the earth—in Bombay, India. Bombay is home to an estimated 300,000 drug addicts in a city of more than 14 million—it is one of the most densely populated cities of the world. In some areas, as many as 1,500 people live within one square mile! The Lord called Reverend J.J. Devaraj, as sweet and dedicated a man of God as one will ever meet, to this city and to the millions of desperate street people who live on her streets. He is the founder and director of Bombay Teen Challenge.

Devaraj, along with a doctor who works full time with him, operates a day care center to minister physical and spiritual healing to drug addicts, street people, prostitutes (both teens and *children*), and abandoned children. When I saw the small facility and tiny staff, and the resources they have in the face of seemingly insurmountable needs, I felt they were, and are, trying to empty an ocean with a bucket.

But every day they open their center and go out on the streets, they come back with another bucket full of souls.

Thanks to John Macey, the Teen Challenge Director in Wales, Great Britain, Bombay now has a Teen Challenge residential center. Macey's center and ministry adopted Bombay and took on the task of raising the money to purchase a home outside the city where young men are being delivered from drugs and discipled. (That doesn't mean Teen Challenge in Wales has lots of money, for they don't; but they realize that their potential to help is greater than India's ability to provide the necessary resources. They took a step of faith and have taken Bombay on as a mission's project. It is my prayer that such stronger ministries in the West will adopt other Teen Challenges in Third World countries.)

Brother Devaraj has his hands full just in reaching drug addicts with the gospel, but now he is recycling his converts and training them to reach out to some of the 100,000 *children* who have been abandoned and are living on the streets.

When I first heard this, I thought, *Oh no, Brother Devaraj, you have more than enough to do with the addicts. Why take on this additional responsibility?* Then it hit me! Who is better able and motivated to reach out to the street children than those who know what life is like on the streets? They know what it is like to be diseased, sick, and starving. Many of the addicts were themselves children who were left on the streets, and who graduated into drug addiction.

As I write these words, the Bombay Teen Challenge is planning to open a "Children's Rescue and Placement Center" where the children of prostitutes, along with other abandoned children, will be fed and bathed, and receive medical and spiritual ministry. These children will stay for about six months, while the center seeks permanent placement for these children with loving families and nurturing Christian homes. Some of these have run away from home and hopefully will be restored to their parents. This center for children will be staffed with the Teen Challenge graduates.

The red light district of Bombay houses approximately 100,000 prostitutes. Five out of every 1,000 Indians above the age of five are infected with tuberculosis. There are an estimated 150,000 TB sufferers in Bombay—more than twice the national average! More than 50 percent of the street people passing through the Bombay Teen Challenge Center have tuberculosis!

Devaraj told us, "Sometimes I wish we did not have to do all this. I wish there were no addicts, no prostitutes, and no street children. [Yet] the Lord has called us to reach them, and He has put within our hearts His love by His Spirit. So we can say the Lord is doing this through us." Brother Devaraj speaks not only for the challenge to his city of Bombay, but for Teen Challenge directors and staff worldwide.

Is the cross still mightier than the switchblade? In some small way I hoped I've answered that question. I also pray that if the reader has family, friends, or acquaintances caught in the hellish grip of drugs or alcohol, that some of the stories I've shared will inspire hope. I pray too that they will lead more addicts to enter a Teen Challenge Center in some part of the world to find a new life in Jesus Christ.

Epilogue

My brother in his epilogue of *The Cross and the Switchblade* wrote, "The story, of course, is far from over."

It seems strange, nearly 40 years after the first center opened, that the very same words are appropriate. Who could have foreseen the devastating scope of the drug problem, and youth upheaval, worldwide?

Never has there been a more important time in history for Teen Challenge to be a center that offers freedom from life-controlling problems. Thus I have a word for those involved in this ministry. When anyone asks, "Who's in charge here?" let your answer be the same as my brother's when he was asked that question years ago: "The Holy Spirit is in charge here."

"As long as He remains in charge, the program will thrive. The minute we try to do things by our own power, we will fail.

"We should write it for all to see in the lintels of every doorway we build. But since that might seem like so many words, we will do better: We will write it in our lives, and in all the lives we can reach out and touch and inspire with the living Spirit of God."

David Wilkerson

The requests for new Teen Challenge Centers across America and around the world continue in countries such as Romania, Croatia, Sibera, Belize, and West Indies; and in major cities such as Moscow, Prague, Beirut, Tel Aviv, and others. In addition, seven major cities in India are being targeted as strategic places for a center. A more recent call comes from China to work with its runaway and delinquent youth.

I believe the next great challenge in America and around the world that awaits the Church in general and Teen Challenge in particular is in ministering to homeless children and wandering lost adolescents. It is a problem of epidemic proportions that very few notice. Yet they are the "plants" and "corner stones" the Psalmist refers to (144:12)—waiting for a family to live and grow in. The "family of God" is their only salvation.

If you would like to send an offering to help in the worldwide mission of Teen Challenge, make your checks payable to "Teen Challenge International" and send it to the address below:

Don Wilkerson
Teen Challenge International
P.O. Box 745
Locust Grove, VA 22508

Books to help you grow strong in Jesus

RIGHT OR RECONCILED
by Joseph L. Garlington.
The message of reconciliation that the Church must declare is simple yet profound: "God is not holding your sins against you!" This is the belief of Joseph L. Garlington, Sr., pastor of a large multiracial congregation in Pittsburgh. Whether you are concerned about racial, gender, or denominational reconciliation, this book is for you. You will never see reconciliation in the same light again!
ISBN 0-7684-2004-0

WORSHIP: THE PATTERN OF THINGS IN HEAVEN
by Joseph L. Garlington.
Worship and praise play a crucial role in the local church. Whether you are a pastor, worship leader, musician, or lay person, you'll find rich and anointed teaching from the Scriptures about worship! Joseph L. Garlington, Sr., a pastor, worship leader, and recording artist in his own right, shows how *worship is the pattern of things in Heaven*!
ISBN 1-56043-195-4

LET ME LIVE AGAIN
by Rev. Angel Nuññez.
One day, Angel met the Lord Jesus Christ, who gave him a new life and a reason to live it. Angel found that the Lord was faithful, even to see him through the trials of his early ministry and the loss of his wife and children, because at his moment of deepest despair, Angel turned to God and cried out, "Take away this pain, and please...let me live again!"
ISBN 1-56043-310-8

POT LIQUOR
by Dr. Millicent Thompson.
Did you know that you can learn more about life over a "bowl of collard greens and some good conversation" than you can learn on a therapist's couch? Hidden in shared stories and passed-down advice are life lessons that you can learn from without experiencing the pain. Like a full course spiritual meal, *Pot Liquor* is guaranteed to feed your soul and keep you coming back for more!
ISBN 1-56043-301-9

Available at your local Christian bookstore.

**For more information and sample chapters,
visit www.reapernet.com**

5B-1:26

Books to help you grow strong in Jesus

THE QUITTING POINT
by Michael Amico.
The ups and downs of life can be compared to the ups and downs of a marathon race—it has many opportunities to quit! In this book Mike Amico, an internationally known evangelist and speaker who also is a competitive long-distance runner, encourages you to persevere through life's pressures, problems, and pain. Don't become another statistic—persevere through to be a winner!
ISBN 1-56043-307-8

WHERE WAS GOD WHEN I CRIED?
by Kay Twombley.
"Why can't I trust God like others do?" "Where is my faith?" "Why don't I hear God as well as others?" If these are questions that linger in your soul, then don't miss this sensitive, healing book. Here Kay Twombley, a licensed professional counselor, helps you remove any obstacles lingering from past, hidden pain and find healing and understanding.
ISBN 1-56043-304-3

PRINCIPLES, PROMISES & POWER
by William V. Thompson.
Are you struggling financially? This essential book highlights 105 biblical principles about finances—principles that are designed by God to take you from "not enough" to "more than enough"! In it you'll learn how to turn your bills into income, defeat debt, tap your "well" for undiscovered money, and much more! Don't miss this powerful and insightful book by the founder of one of the most sought-after personal money management firms on the U.S. East Coast!
ISBN 1-56043-308-6

DISCOVER YOUR PURPOSE! DESIGN YOUR DESTINY! DIRECT YOUR ACHIEVEMENT!
by William D. Greenman.
Do you know your purpose in life? Do you need some help in achieving your life's goals? Don't miss this book! Here the author presents practical, time-tested principles to help you find God's plan for your life—and to fulfill it! Get prepared—your life is about to change!
ISBN 0-7684-2009-1

Available at your local Christian bookstore.

For more information and sample chapters, visit www.reapernet.com

5B-1:27

Exciting titles
by Jim & Michal Ann Goll

— FATHER, FORGIVE US!
by Jim W. Goll.
What is holding back a worldwide "great awakening"? What hinders the Church all over the world from rising up and bringing in the greatest harvest ever known? The answer is simple: sin! God is calling Christians today to take up the mantle of identificational intercession and repent for the sins of the present and past; for the sins of our fathers; for the sins of the nations. Will you heed the call? This book shows you how!
ISBN 0-7684-2025-3

— WOMEN ON THE FRONT LINES
by Michal Ann Goll.
History is filled with ordinary women who have changed the course of their generation. Here Michal Ann Goll, co-founder of Ministry to the Nations with her husband, Jim, shares how her own life was transformed and highlights nine women whose lives will impact yours! Every generation faces the same choices and issues; learn how you, too, can heed the call to courage and impact a generation.
ISBN 0-7684-2020-2

— ENCOUNTERS WITH A SUPERNATURAL GOD
by Jim and Michal Ann Goll.
The Golls know that angels are real. They have firsthand experience with supernatural angelic encounters. In this book you'll read and learn about angels and supernatural manifestations of God's Presence—and the real encounters that both Jim and Michal Ann have had! As the founders of Ministry to the Nations and speakers and teachers, they share that God wants to be intimate friends with His people. Go on an adventure with the Golls and find out if God has a supernatural encounter for you!
ISBN 1-56043-199-7

— THE LOST ART OF INTERCESSION
by Jim W. Goll.
Finally there is something that really explains what is happeninng to so many folk in the Body of Christ. What does it mean to carry the burden of the Lord? Where is it in Scripture and in history? Why do I feel as though God is groaning within me? No, you are not crazy; God is restoring genuine intercessory prayer in the hearts of those who are open to respond to His burden and His passion.
ISBN 1-56043-697-2

Available at your local Christian bookstore.

For more information and sample chapters, visit www.reapernet.com

5B-1:28

Books to help you grow strong in Jesus

► THE MARTYRS' TORCH

by Bruce Porter.

In every age of history, darkness has threatened to extinguish the light. But also in every age of history, heroes and heroines of the faith rose up to hold high the torch of their testimony—witnesses to the truth of the gospel of Jesus Christ. On a fateful spring day at Columbine High, others lifted up their torches and joined the crimson path of the martyrs' way. We cannot forget their sacrifice. A call is sounding forth from Heaven: "Who will take up the martyrs' torch which fell from these faithful hands?" Will you?

ISBN 0-7684-2046-6

► THE YOUNG WARRIORS

by Wesley Smith.

Today more than ever believers need to rise up and be people of courage in service to God! Here Wesley Smith, president of Full Life Crusade and a popular lecturer, Bible teacher, youth speaker, and missions leader, tells you what it takes to be a warrior in God's army and to slay the giants arrayed against the Church: the ability to hear God, then obey! God needs you in this end-time harvest to fulfill the Great Commission!

ISBN 1-56043-296-9

► WHAT GOD DID FOR ME, HE CAN DO FOR YOU

by Erlie Lenz Cesar.

Erlie Lenz Cesar's life story is a testimony to the power and mercy of God that are available to His people if they will but ask. Healed from severe asthma as a child, his eyesight restored to both eyes after failed operations, successful in business ventures—these are just a few of the stories Senhor Cesar can tell of God's goodness in his life. A highly respected Christian businessman and owner of an industrial plant in his native Brazil, Erlie Lenz Cesar testifies that no matter what obstacle, problem, or illness you face, what God did for him, He can do for you!

ISBN 1-56043-328-0

► VALLEY OF TROUBLE, MOUNTAIN OF HOPE

by David Davis.

David was a successful actor and instructor in New York. His career was great—except something was missing. What? He found his answer in the saving love of Jesus Christ. After being mentored at Times Square Church under David Wilkerson, David felt called to Israel. Today, David and his wife, Karen, minister to both Jewish and Arab drug addicts in Israel. Their enthralling testimony of God's work in their lives and in their ministry in Israel will help you to persevere through to fulfilling God's plan for your own life!

ISBN 1-56043-336-1

Available at your local Christian bookstore.

For more information and sample chapters, visit www.reapernet.com

5B-1:29